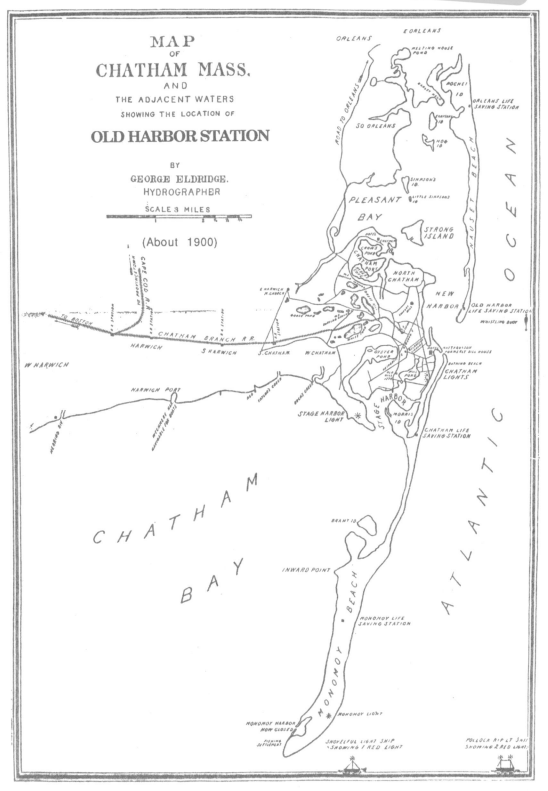

MAP
OF
CHATHAM MASS.
AND
THE ADJACENT WATERS
SHOWING THE LOCATION OF
OLD HARBOR STATION
BY
GEORGE ELDRIDGE.
HYDROGRAPHER
SCALE 3 MILES

(About 1900)

This book is dedicated
to the brave and skilled men
of the U.S. Life Saving Service
and
the U.S. Coast Guard
who served at Old Harbor Station.
We must never forget their sacrifices,
dedication, and perseverance.

Seashore Sentinel:

The Old Harbor Lifesaving Station

on Cape Cod

Richard G. Ryder

Richard G. Ryder

Published by Lifesaving Service Markers

Copyright 2009 Richard G. Ryder
All rights reserved.
Published 2009.
First Edition.

West Barnstable Press
ISBN 0-9816873-4-6

Library of Congress Control Number:
2009929487

To purchase a copy of this book, contact:
Richard G. Ryder
330 Silver Spring Beach Road
Eastham, Massachusetts 02642-1815

www.uslifesavingmarker.com

Seashore Sentinel:

The Old Harbor Lifesaving Station on Cape Cod

Table Of Contents

Introduction

Old Harbor Lifesaving Station stands watch over the sands of Cape Cod as it has since 1898. It was home ten months of the year for the rugged men of the U.S. Life Saving Service and year round for the U.S. Coast Guardsmen. They kept a sharp lookout and patrolled the surf edges in all kinds of weather, looking for shipwrecks, survivors, and saboteurs.

Old Harbor Life Saving Station was built in Chatham, Cape Cod, Massachusetts in 1897 and first occupied in March 1898. It was officially decommissioned and closed by the U.S. Coast Guard on July 1, 1944. It was later sold to owners who used it as a fishing camp and guest lodge. The building was threatened, however, by coastal erosion and since it was located within the boundaries of the Cape Cod National Seashore, the National Park Service purchased it in 1973. In November of 1977, the building was divided into two parts, lifted off its foundation by two large cranes, swung out to a barge on the Atlantic Ocean beach, and floated to Provincetown Harbor. The timing was perfect, as a February storm, the "Blizzard of '78", washed over the site and certainly would have claimed the building if it had remained there. In 1978, the building was taken off the barge and reassembled on its present site on National Seashore land near Race Point. It is open for visitors in the summer, and Breeches Buoy demonstrations that include firing of the Lyle gun are given every Thursday evening in July and August. The Park Service has drawn up extensive plans for furnishing the building with items similar, if not identical, to those used by the men of the U.S. Life Saving Service in 1902. Restoration work is ongoing. The information included in this book should assist and encourage the National Park Service, The Friends of the Cape Cod National Seashore, and private individuals in that endeavor.

There have been a lot of books written on the exploits of the men of the Life Saving Service, and the Annual Reports of the U.S. Life Saving Service have excellent descriptions of wrecks where life was lost. I wrote about the station in 1990 in a now out-of-print book called "Old Harbor Station – Cape Cod". I have used some of that timeless information in this book, and have added new photographs. I expanded the Coast Guard coverage in a separate chapter entitled "The Coast Guard Era". Information about the *ORCUTT* wreck, Life Saving Service history, a 1904 week at the station, private occupancy, and moving the station has been included to make the story of the station as complete as possible. I think it is important to keep alive the history and traditions of a proud and brave group of men.

Richard G. Ryder, North Eastham, Massachusetts, 2009

A Brief History of the U.S. Revenue Cutter Service and the U.S. Life Saving Service

After the Revolutionary War, the Continental Navy was disbanded. There was no sea force available for the protection of the coasts and the maritime interests of the newly constituted United States until the organization of the Revenue Cutter Service, approved by President Washington on August 4th, 1790. The duties of the Service eventually consisted of the search for possible contraband of all merchant vessels arriving within the United States; suppression of piracy; the search for wrecked or missing vessels; the enforcement of neutrality laws; the suppression of mutiny; the protection of seal and other fisheries in Alaska; the enforcement of the navigation laws; the patrol of the ice fields and the destruction of derelicts in the North Atlantic Ocean; extending medical and surgical aid to the crews of American vessels engaged in the deep sea fisheries. Not lastly, but important to readers of this book, is the fact that officers of the Revenue Cutter Service were involved in the formation of the U.S. Life Saving Service.

(Source: a 1915 U.S. Government Printing Office pamphlet entitled "United States Revenue-Cutter Service". In other official publications it was referred to as "The Revenue Marine Service" or "Revenue Marine Bureau".)

Postcard, author's collection

Revenue Cutter Service Cadets alongside a cutter at the school
near Baltimore, MD

The history of the U.S. Life-Saving Service on Cape Cod starts with the organization of the Massachusetts Humane Society by a few benevolent persons in 1786. In an attempt to alleviate the miseries of shipwreck victims, small huts were built in 1789 on desolate portions of the coast of Massachusetts. The first building of this type was erected on Lovell's Island near Boston. In 1807, the Society established the first lifeboat station at Cohasset. In 1849, some Federal Government money was spent by the Humane Society in erecting houses of refuge on Cape Cod. After some terrible shipwrecks had occurred on the coast of New Jersey, Congress appropriated $10,000 for providing surfboats and other appliances for use on that coast. Soon, twenty-two station houses were erected on the coasts of New Jersey and Long Island. In 1850, Congress appropriated $20,000 for "Life-Saving purposes." Half of the money was spent for stations on Long Island and for one at Watch Hill, Rhode Island. The other half of the money was spent for lifeboats and boathouses on the Carolina, Georgia, Florida and Texas coasts. The stations had volunteer crews and were successful in saving lives, but there was no effective control over them. Some of the boats and much of the gear was stolen or improperly used.

Revenue Cutter Service Cadets at Drill with Breech Loading Rifle

On April 20, 1871, Congress appropriated $200,000 and authorized the Secretary of the Treasury to employ crews of paid surfmen at the stations for such periods as he might deem necessary. That same year, Sumner Increase Kimball, a lawyer from Maine, became the head of the Revenue Marine Bureau of the Treasury Department. The Revenue Marine had charge of the life-saving stations. After taking over, Mr. Kimball saw to it that he or Capt. John Faunce inspected all of the stations. What they found was shocking. Buildings were in disrepair, apparatus was broken or otherwise unusable, articles had been stolen,

Revenue Cutter Service Cadets at Pistol Drill, ca 1904

and some Keepers were not living anywhere near their stations. Mr. Kimball proceeded to work tirelessly on reorganizing the Bureau. Keepers were appointed based on skill, rather than political affiliation. Incompetent surfmen were discharged, and rigorous training and inspection systems were setup. There was never enough money to do the work required; in fact the appropriation for 1877-78 was so far below normal, that the stations were not opened until the 1st of December. The tragic loss of 98 persons from the stranding on the North Carolina coast of the steamer *HURON*, just six days before the stations were to open, brought an outcry from the public. By 1879, adequate money was appropriated, and the Life-Saving Service became a separate establishment, rather than a branch of the Revenue Marine Bureau. Mr. Kimball was nominated by the President and unanimously confirmed by the Congress as the General Superintendent of the U.S. Life-Saving Service. The number of lives and the amount of property saved increased each year, and public support was high. In June 1872, Congress had authorized the construction of nine stations on Cape Cod. The following stations were built in the winter of 1872: Race Point and Peaked Hill Bars at Provincetown; the Highlands station at North Truro; Pamet River at Truro; Cahoon Hollow at Wellfleet; Nauset Station at North Eastham; Orleans in East Orleans; Chatham at Chatham near Morris Island (and later on moved to two miles North of Chatham Twin Lights); and Monomoy Station on Monomoy Island. Later on, four more stations were built on Cape Cod. The High Head Station, built and manned in 1883, was located between the Highland Station and the Peaked Hill Bars Station. The Wood End Station located in Provincetown and facing Cape Cod Bay, was built in 1896 and manned in 1897. Old Harbor Station in Chatham was built in 1897 and manned in 1898. The Monomoy

Point Station, located at the South end of Monomoy Island, was built and manned in 1902. By 1903, there were 13 stations operating on the coast of Cape Cod. The Town of Chatham, with four stations within its boundaries, probably had more stations than any other town in the country. **In January 1915, the Revenue Marine Service and the Life-Saving Service were combined and named the U.S. Coast Guard.** General Superintendent Kimball retired at this time, having performed his duty in a most admirable fashion for over 43 years.

The stations continued in use for varying numbers of years, but with the coming of helicopters and sophisticated electronics, surfboats and beach apparatus carts were no longer needed. Many stations were closed after World War II ended, as there were not enough men left on active duty to man them. The last use of the breeches buoy apparatus for rescue purposes on Cape Cod (and probably in the United States) was on January 16, 1962. The *MARGARET ROSE* came ashore near Wood End in Provincetown. Coast Guard rescuers safely removed seven men from the wreck.

In 2009, the only Life-Saving station on Cape Cod remaining in its original configuration is Old Harbor Station, and it is not located where it was originally built. The Coast Guard remains very important to Cape Cod fishermen and recreational boaters. The sea is still prone to be violent, powerful, and uncompromising. The Life-Saving Service and the Revenue Cutter Service, in the form of today's dedicated Coast Guard men and women, continues on.

CHAPTER 2

Early Cape Cod Lifesavers

The original nine Life Saving Stations on Cape Cod were built and manned shortly after the Civil War. They were called Red Houses, as they had their roofs painted red so that vessels in distress could identify them and maybe beach nearby. The coast was very sparsely inhabited at that time, and perhaps if the shipwreck victims knew there was a place of solace close by, they could strike out for it. The men who manned these stations were not volunteers. They were paid to be on duty for ten months a year, at a rate initially of $65 a month. There were no benefits. They had to provide their own food, and cook it themselves.

The first nine stations were at Race Point, Peaked Hill Bar, Highland, Pamet River, Cahoon Hollow, Nauset, Orleans, Chatham, and Monomoy. They were identical in design and construction. They had been built on a plan drawn up in 1871 by an architect in the employ of the U.S. Life-Saving Service. All told, there were 71 of these Red House stations built in the United States. In addition to the nine on the Cape, one was built on Block Island, RI, 23 on Long Island, NY, and 38 along the coast of New Jersey.

The 1872 *Annual Report of the Revenue Marine Bureau* contains a detailed description of these Red House stations: "All these houses have been constructed under plans and specifications carefully prepared with a view to durability, and affording proper accommodations for the apparatus and the means of providing comfortable protection of the crews and relief to those who may be rescued from shipwreck. They are 42 feet long by 18 feet wide, and each contains a lower and an attic story. Each story is divided into two apartments. The boats, a wagon, and other heavy apparatus occupy the large apartment below, while the smaller one is a living room for the crew, provided with conveniences for cooking. Above, one room is for the small articles of apparatus, and the other is provided with several cot-beds and suitable bedding."

Of course there were only outside toilet facilities, no running water, no telephones or electricity. No one had these amenities at that time, so living conditions at these stations were only challenging in that they were far removed from town.

Local men, six or seven plus the Keeper at each one, manned the Cape stations. Chatham and Orleans stations might have had men from Harwich, Brewster, Dennis, Orleans and Chatham in their crew makeup. In the 1890s, members of the nearby King Hiram Masonic Lodge primarily manned the Provincetown area stations. The stations in between also used local men to their advantage, and credit.

Illustration by Harold M. Brett, *Life-savers on Old Malabar* from *Harper's Monthly* 1907

THE DUNES OF MONOMOY

The Keepers initially were chosen from the ranks of local sea captains, members of the Massachusetts Humane Society, or other experienced seamen. Later on, they were promoted from the ranks of the most able surfmen. The surfmen were selected based on their skill in handling small boats, their reliability, and their willingness to do arduous duty. There were obvious advantages in having men who were familiar with the local waters and whose attributes and shortcomings the Keeper knew. If they didn't work out for any reason, they were discharged immediately. The men who were let go had no recourse – no grievance procedures were known. It was probably just as well, as there was no room for men who couldn't pull their oar, and little time for discussion.

CHAPTER 3

The Wreck of the *Calvin B. Orcutt*

The four masted coasting schooner *CALVIN B. ORCUTT* left Portland, Maine on December 22, 1896, bound for Norfolk, Virginia with no cargo aboard. Captain George Bailey owned her. The master on what proved to be her last voyage was Captain Edgar Pearce of Manasquan, New Jersey. She carried a crew of at least eight men. The New England Shipbuilding Company at Bath, Maine built her in 1888 with a length of 189 feet, a beam of 40 feet and a draft of 18 ¹/₂ feet with her centerboard down.

Schooner CALVIN B. ORCUTT, 953 Tons. Capt. GEORGE BAILEY.
Built by NEW ENGLAND SHIP BUILDING COMPANY, Bath, Maine. Launched May 10, 1888.

Photograph by J. C. Higgins, Bath, Maine; courtesy of the Chatham Historical (MA) Society

On December 23rd, the *ORCUTT* ran into a Northeast blizzard while off the backside (Easterly side) of Cape Cod. During a lull in the storm, at around 3:30 pm, Jonathan Eldredge, a fisherman from North Chatham, looked out from his fish shanty at Ministers Point and saw a schooner just coming to anchor off the outside beach North of the harbor entrance. At that time, the harbor entrance was just about opposite what is now the Chatham Fish Pier. Mr. Eldredge could see her pitching and straining in the heavy seas. Sails were set only on the two after masts, and while Mr. Eldredge watched, the more forward sail was hauled down and furled, or tied to the boom. The vessel was lost to sight when it started to snow again, but not before Eldredge had called attention to the vessel's predicament to Fred W. Nickerson, Jr. and two other fishermen close by. In a short time the group had risen to 11 men, all hardy fishermen and boatmen. Fred Nickerson had served in the Life Saving Service at the Chatham Station and knew from the position of the *ORCUTT* and the heavy sea state that soon she would either pound her bottom out on the sand shoals under her or drag onto the beach. Either way, her crew was doomed to die with the vessel unless aid could reach them quickly.

The vessel lay at the southern end of the territory of Orleans Station, but the men there had no knowledge of the wreck. Fisherman Nickerson knew that the telephone cable from the Chatham station to the Orleans station had been inoperative for several weeks. He proposed that he and his companions launch a nearby pilot boat and row across Pleasant Bay to the Orleans Station and report what they had seen. None of the men would agree to go, as the weather was apparently very severe. The group agreed to try the trip at 7:30 that evening if the weather had moderated enough. Nickerson determined to get the news of the wreck to the Orleans station before that time, however, and set off with a companion on a three-mile trip for the telegraph office at Chatham. They arrived there about 6 pm and immediately sent off a wire to Mr. Small, the Marine Observer at Highland Light in Truro, who manned the nearest office connected with the Life Saving Service lines. The line between Highland Light and Orleans was down also, so no warning could be sent by that means.

Nickerson remembered that there was a telephone connection between the Life Saving Service District Superintendent's home in East Orleans and the Orleans Life Saving Station. At his suggestion, the telegraph operator in the Orleans railroad depot, Miss Amelia Snow, was requested to send a messenger with the news to the Superintendent in East Orleans. She said she'd try to find someone to carry the message. In the meantime, Nickerson telephoned Keeper Doane of the Chatham Station and told him of the situation. Fisherman Nickerson returned to his home in North Chatham at about 8 pm, now convinced that it would be impossible to row across Pleasant Bay to Orleans Station. The wind had not moderated and he was no doubt tired from the trip to Chatham and back. The reader needs to be aware that, unlike today, there were many open fields, very few trees and not many houses on the Cape during the 1890s. There was little protection from the wind, and even a moderate wind driven snowfall could yield deep drifts in places. Keeper Hezekiah Doane of the Chatham Station, located on the North end of Monomoy, was now aware of the vessel's dilemma but was also powerless to effect a rescue from his station because of the heavy seas. He knew from experience that it would be almost impossible to transport a surfboat and beach apparatus cart across the cut-through to the mainland and then over roads covered with deep snow to the upper part of Chatham Harbor.

Then they would have to cross the harbor to the outside beach, an even greater task. He also knew that, with the wind veering more to the North each hour, the schooner, or her wreckage, would be likely to drift southward onto the beach near his station. He determined that he and his crew should stay at their station. He directed his men to keep a sharp lookout for signs of the wreck and report directly to him if they found any sign of it. At 10:40 pm the South patrolman telephoned from a point 2 1/4 miles away that he had found a vessel's battered yawl boat in the surf. Keeper Doane then called out all his men and started southward along the beach to see what else was washing up on the shore. About a half-mile below the station they began to find pieces of wreckage, including a broken quarter board with the lettering *CALVIN B. OR* on it. Nearby they met the South patrolman who reported no further wreckage beyond that point. They all returned to the station. At five the next morning Keeper Doane took his men to a point on the beach opposite the bars, deeming it advisable to be there just in case, but there was nothing in view but the raging surf. Back in Orleans, Miss Snow was unable to find anyone to carry the message to Superintendent Benjamin C. Sparrow's home in East Orleans until about 10 pm. A livery stable keeper had said he would not allow one of his horses out in that weather "for love or money". One young man offered to go for five dollars, but because no one could be found who would pay him, he didn't make the try. The local express man agreed to go after his day's work was done, but he would be delayed because the storm had slowed the train and disrupted his business.

Finally, Henry K. Cummings, a young Orleans merchant, heard of the emergency and volunteered to deliver the message. It took Mr. Cummings an hour to reach Mr. Sparrow's home. Carrying a lantern, he had waded through drifts up to four feet deep. The wind was at near hurricane strength, especially up on the higher ground. Mr. Sparrow immediately called Keeper James H. Charles of the Orleans Life Saving Station on the phone and told him what was known of the vessel in distress to the South of the station. He told the Keeper he would join him as soon as he could. Keeper Charles and his crew dug the snow from the boat room doors, took the beach apparatus cart around to the lee of the station and hitched it to the station horse. At 12:20 am, Keeper Charles and his crew set out on the inside road along the marsh, as the surf on the outer beach was running up over the beach to the dunes. The snow was nearly knee deep and very wet. At 2:25 am they discovered the vessel about 4 1/4 miles from Orleans station. The nearly exhausted horse was led to the Chatham Station barn, which had not been moved when the station was moved back to the mainland. The *ORCUTT* lay about 600 yards off shore, with her bow pointed to the Northeast. The masts still stood but the hull was submerged. In between snow squalls the Surfmen could see, by the moonlight, the gaffs and booms with the sails furled upon them. The exception was the spanker, or fourth mast, which had its sail set with a double reef. The Surfmen saw no signs of life in the rigging. A short time later, a huge sea crashed into the middle of the sail and split it from top to bottom. Keeper Charles walked downwind from the wreck to listen for cries from survivors, but heard none. He could see that the masts were no longer in line, which meant the ship was breaking up. He started up the beach to get the apparatus cart when he met Superintendent Sparrow, who had just arrived. Before they got back to the cart, the foremast fell and dragged the three remaining masts down with it. Before dawn it was decided the wreck had finally been driven far enough towards the beach, so an attempt should be made to try to reach it with the Lyle gun and breeches buoy. There was not much hope that anyone could still be alive, but the lifesavers fired a shot, with line attached, over the wreck. The line quickly became entangled in the wreckage and parted. Further attempts at rescue were not made. After daybreak, many people arrived by boat from Chatham. Keeper Doane and his crew came in their surfboat after a hard pull from Monomoy. After patrolling the beach to the South of the wreck for bodies and not finding any, the crews of both stations packed up their gear and returned to their stations. Superintendent Sparrow left the scene at 4:30 am, reaching home at 9:30, having walked all the way home. The Life Saving crews were accused of cowardice by newspapers in Boston and New Jersey, but an official investigation later showed that both Keepers had taken the proper action.

Benjamin C. Sparrow

The trip that the 57-year-old Superintendent Sparrow made that stormy night was nothing shy of remarkable. He traveled some seven miles, often in waist deep wet snow, in total darkness, across a landscape in which the snow obliterated every identifiable object along the way. The journey just about exhausted him, and much later his eyesight was still seriously impaired from the experience. A younger and more fit Mr. Cummings had to lay down in the snow three times to rest on his way back from the Superintendent's home. Mr. Sparrow had made it to nearly every wreck that occurred in his territory in the past, but this one was probably the hardest on him.

For his efforts, Mr. Cummings received a Letter of Commendation and a reward from Sumner I. Kimball, General Superintendent of the U.S. Life Saving Service. For Mr. Sparrow, it was his perceived duty, and he did it.

In a January 4th, 1897 article in the *Barnstable Patriot*, it was written "The Chatham Bar whistling buoy has been gone from its proper position since Dec. 16th, and in its present position (about one mile SW by W from station) is a very dangerous menace to navigation, as vessels running their course either way from it will run upon the shoals. Had it been in true position, Hydrographer Geo. W. Eldredge thinks, it is probable the wreck of the ill-fated schr. *CALVIN B. ORCUTT* would never have happened."

Four masted schooner similar to the *CALVIN B. ORCUTT*

Construction of Old Harbor Life Saving Station (No. 41) was speeded up in 1897 because of this wreck. The distance that Orleans Life Saving Station had to cover was too great and the Chatham Station was too far away to be useful for wrecks on the outer beach. In the late 1870s, the original Chatham station had been moved across the harbor to the Old Harbor Station site. It remained there a few years but had been moved back to its original site southerly of Chatham Lights. When this station was moved from the Old Harbor site, it was believed that a new station would be built there as soon as money could be appropriated. After the wreck of the *ORCUTT* in December 1896, money was found and the planned Old Harbor Station was built. It became operational in March 1898, with Captain Hezekiah Doane as the first Keeper. Six Surfmen were on duty as of the 1st of May 1898.

(Most of the information in this chapter was taken from an article written by Holman H. Spence that appeared in the November 25th, 1977 issue of The Cape Codder *newspaper. It, in turn, came from the* Annual Report of the U.S. Life Saving Service for 1896.*)*

CHAPTER 4

Description of
Old Harbor Life Saving Station

Old Harbor Station was originally built and located in the Town of Chatham, in Barnstable County, on the outer "elbow" of Cape Cod, Massachusetts. George R. Tolman, an architectural draftsman assigned to the Life Saving Service, designed the main building of the station in 1894. The type of station was known as the "Duluth" type, as the first of fifteen constructed between 1894 and 1904 was built at Duluth, Minnesota. One of these was erected at Wood End, in Provincetown, in 1896, ironically not too far from the present location of Old Harbor Station. The site for what eventually became known as Station #41 was selected by Captain J.B. Moore, a Superintendent of Construction for the Revenue Cutter Service, Superintendent Sparrow of the Life Saving Service, and Keeper Hezekiah Doane of the Chatham Life Saving Station while visiting the beach on July 9, 1897. The position of the station was estimated to be at a point about five miles from the Orleans station and about ³/₄ mile South of the former site of the Chatham station. The Latitude and Longitude were later determined to be 41°41'45" N, 69°56' 00" W. The land the station was built on was part of 4.5 acres donated to the Federal Government. Several names considered for the station were "Mud Hole" and "Strong Island", with "Old Harbor" the final choice. The site could best be described as desolate, wind blown sand dunes.

Old Harbor Life Saving Station, Chatham, Mass.

Postcard, author's collection

There were no rocks at all in the area; the largest stones would fit in your pocket. Fresh water could be obtained by driving a well point down through the beach sand to the "lens" of potable water that lay just above the salt water level. All fresh water used at the station ultimately came from rainwater. Vegetation in the area near the station consisted of Beach Grass, Dusty Miller, Tall Wormwood, Beach Peas, Salt-Spray Roses, Poverty Grass, Bayberries, and Beach Plums. Animal life consisted of a naturally balanced population of field mice, skunks, weasels, foxes, and rabbits. Hawks, owls, gulls and crows visited year round. A wide variety of migratory birds either visited for short periods or passed by on their journeys. The new station was to be built by J. S. Randall of Portland, Maine, at a contract price of $4,437.52. The actual construction work is thought to have been accomplished by Mr. David Edwards of Chatham. Construction must have started immediately after the site was chosen, as the building was occupied only eight months later.

The specifications for painting the exterior of the building called for cornices, trimmings, moldings, casings, the piazza and porch posts, railings, steps, and porch and piazza ceilings to be painted with three coats of French gray; the doors and remainder of the outside work to be a light colonial yellow; the outside of window sashes to be blue-black; and the shingles to be left natural. A sign denoting "U.S. Life Saving Station" was mounted on the roof over the boat room doors. The 8" letters were to be black on a colonial yellow background, with a contrasting French gray border. Later on during the Coast Guard era, the roof was painted red and the exterior walls were painted white. Green paint was used for blinds, doors, and sashes. Light lead color paint was used for porch floors, treads of outside steps, and for repainting interior floors. This color scheme is still in use at active Coast Guard stations today.

The "station" was made up of the boathouse, main building, stable, several outbuildings, wreck pole, and flagstaff. The station's purpose was to provide a storage place for lifesaving and other equipment, temporary shelter of rescued persons, a place for the crew to eat and sleep, and to provide shelter for the horse. There was no running water, no electricity, no central heat, no refrigeration and no inside plumbing when the station was first occupied. Central heat arrived in 1910, indoor plumbing was installed in 1928, and a 32-volt electric light system was installed in 1933. The crew provided their own food, uniforms, outer clothing, and, until 1917, their own toilet paper. The Life Saving Service provided fuel, a place to live, and a respectable job in the winter when work was difficult to get.

The Boathouse

The boathouse was a one-story gable roofed building separate from the main building. It measured 28' 5" by 14' 3". It was received in the Inventory Log Book on October 22nd, 1900.

Surf Boat Drill, Old Harbor Life S. S., Chatham, Mass.

In 1902, it was located about ½ mile to the Southwest of the station, on the "inside" of North Beach, with a boat ramp leading West towards the bay and the Chatham mainland. It had two large doors that swung outward. It was moved once in late November 1901, and again in 1905. According to Richard Allen Ryder, Surfman Richard E. Ryder's oldest son, each man of the Old Harbor Station crew had a dory that he kept anchored near the boathouse for going back and forth to town on his liberty day.

In the 1950s, this building still had its rough boathouse interior, with a hand pump for water and a wood stove for heat. The capstan, for hauling boats up the ramp and into the building, was still bolted to the floor. The building was privately owned and used as a weekend retreat until it was washed away in the "Perfect Storm" in late October of 1991. It had been in use for 85 years.

Surf Boat Drill, Old Harbor Life S. S., Chatham, Mass.

The Old Harbor surfmen, with rollers used to move the surfboat to the waters of Pleasant Bay

Power surfboat comparable to the one kept near the Boathouse after 1916
(Photo taken near Boston Light, ca 1910, with Surfmen waving
to an early U.S. Navy aircraft from Squantum Naval Air Station)

The Boatroom

The boatroom was the large room located on the North side of Old Harbor Station. It had two pairs of doors that opened east, towards the sea. Each opening was 9' 4" wide. Initially, a wooden ramp led from the doors down to the sand. Later, the wood was replaced by concrete that remained until the mid 1960s. The room was not heated, as there was nothing in the room that would freeze. Being shaded from the sun and having no large windows facing any but late afternoon sun, it probably never got hot inside. The room measured 40 feet long by 24 feet wide. Access from inside the building was through the messroom. There was a loft above the room, where the extra gear was probably stored, reached with the use of a ladder.

Metal "Francis" Life car suspended above a Beach Apparatus Cart

Old Harbor Lifesavers in front of boat room, ca 1914. Surfboat in left bay, beach apparatus cart to right. Keeper Hezekiah F. Doane, 2nd from left

Plans for a similar station at Salisbury Beach, Massachusetts show a roughly 7'x9' door that would have been in the Northwest corner of this room. For a station with two surfboats, this would have been the door by which the Beach Apparatus Cart would have been taken in and out. Old Harbor Station had only one surfboat in the boatroom, the other being kept at the boathouse. Specifications for the boatroom called for the frame inside, including the roof framing, to show, dressed. The floor was of single thickness, three inch thick pine plank, probably southern yellow pine. The partition wall between the main building and the boatroom was to be treated as an outside wall, with boarding and clapboards the full height of the wall. The boatroom walls were not painted, but the inerior doors and window trim were painted a light olive.

This room was the heart of the place, as it was where the surfboat was stored on the boat carriage. Two beach apparatus carts were stored here, as was the life car, and other essential lifesaving gear.

The Bunkroom

The bunkroom was located in the main building on the second floor, directly above the kitchen and messroom. It had inward sloping walls, with the four-flue chimney passing up through the middle of the room. There was provision for connecting a stove to the chimney, and no doubt one of the three Princess Beaver coal stoves received in 1898 was installed in this room. A ventilating flue, which would exhaust built-up heat, was provided near the top of the chimney for use in the summer. There were at least 12 iron beds in the room, with two more in the adjacent guest bedroom in the Northwest corner. The Keeper slept in his quarters on the first floor.

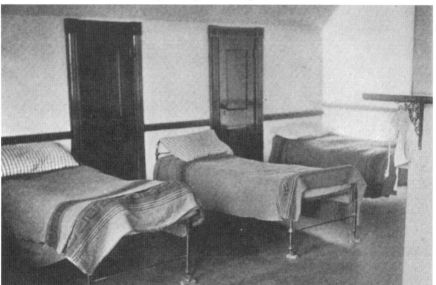

Bunkroom at Cahoon Hollow Station, Wellfleet – about 1902
(There are no known photos of the Old Harbor bunkroom)

In an interview done by a staff member of the Mystic Seaport Museum in April 1978, Rebecca Ryder told of sleeping in the second floor guest room (also known as the Spare Room) when she accompanied her surfman husband at the station during his turn at "cook week". She said it got very cold in the room and, with as many horse blankets as you could put on, it was still hard to keep warm. Normally, seven men would sleep in the bunkroom when the station was manned. The extra beds were there for rescued persons. The men were provided with woolen blankets, mattresses, mattress covers, pillows, pillow covers, and linen sheets when the station opened in 1898. Since there was no inside toilet at the station, the men probably used chamber pots.

Six washbasins were received in 1898, but whether they were used upstairs or not isn't known. Since there were 18 dining chairs in the building, some of them must have been used in the bunkroom. There were lockers for the crew in the second floor hallway. Skilled carpenters of the Cape Cod National Seashore reconstructed the lockers in 2008.

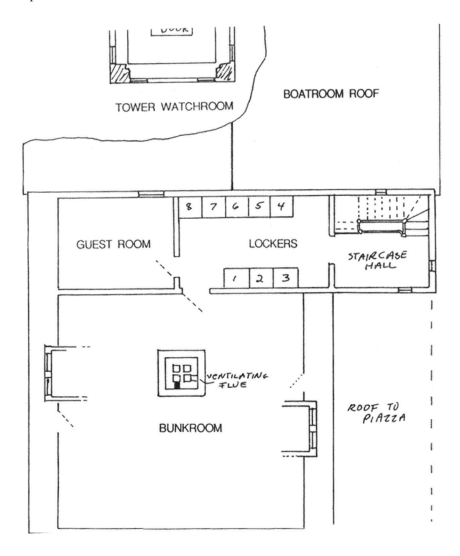

Floor Plan for 2nd floor, Old Harbor Station

The Keeper's Quarters

The Keeper's quarters consisted of two rooms, the larger reached by entering from the back piazza on the west side, by going through the kitchen, or by going through the outer office, which was the smaller. The larger room was the Keeper's living space and the smaller one was where his bookwork and record keeping would have been done. The smaller one could be reached from the hallway that led from the boat-room to the messroom. There was a thimble in the chimney, in the living space, for one of the Princess Beaver coal stoves. All of the Keeper's paperwork was done by hand, with pen and ink, until an L.C. Smith typewriter arrived in September of 1919. The office was furnished with an oak roll top desk and a chair. There were many official books that were kept here, as well as the filled rough logs, old files, office supplies, medicines and bandages, and a safe.

Roll top desk – a major piece of furniture kept in the office.
It was received in 1898.
Desk was described as "Desk, oak, roll top, 4' long, 3'9" high, 30" deep with side closet, mounted on large plate casters".

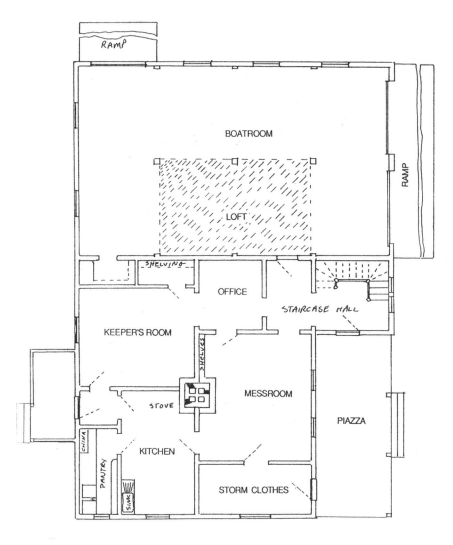

First Floor Layout
Note that the Keeper's Office was readily accessible by the crew without entering his bedroom area.

The Kitchen and Coal Stoves

The kitchen was of great importance at Old Harbor Station. It was essential to the men, as they were involved in an arduous occupation and they burned up a lot of calories in the process. These men had all come from various lives at sea, and were appreciative of a warm, well-equipped place to prepare decent food. The kitchen was located on the first floor of the Southwest corner of the main building. There was a large sink, a hand pump that drew water from a driven well, a table for a work surface, and a large coal stove for cooking. The first stove was a Beaver range, but this was replaced with a Crawford range in 1904. Next to the kitchen was a commodious pantry, with shelving for pots and pans and bins for flour and sugar. Although little is known about what was actually eaten, if one knows what was available to cook, it is not difficult to figure out what the men ate. The station was in a remote location by today's standards, but back then, if it wasn't under sail and moving away from a port, it was not remote. The men were obligated to buy their own food, so if they could get the food themselves along the shores, it was considered money in their pockets. Chatham waters have yielded clams, quahogs, crabs, eels, lobsters, waterfowl and fish for centuries. There is no reason why the men would not have taken advantage of this local bounty. They could get milk, butter, beef, pork, flour, sugar, fresh vegetables in season, and various staples from merchants or farmers in town by taking the station dory (or their own), rowing across Chatham harbor to the Cow Yard, walking to town and buying what they needed. There were frequent trips to be made to Orleans by horse and wagon, so fresh milk was purchased from Asa Mayo's farm in East Orleans. Given the amount of horse manure available, the amount of dried eelgrass for mulch, the good drainage, and the amount of sun and fresh water available, there is reason to believe that the Keeper could have raised vegetables in a garden in the summer. Richard E. Ryder is known to have raised potatoes and at least one turkey at Monomoy Life Saving Station when he was Keeper there. (The 25-pound turkey died a natural death a week before Thanksgiving.) Chickens would have loved scratching in and around where the horse was kept, and as long as foxes and weasels were kept from them, an egg supply was ensured. The crew had to bake his or her own bread, rolls, pies, biscuits and cookies, but back then, everyone did that. They probably ate a lot of chowder, stew, meat and quahog pies, baked beans, and fresh fish. Of course coffee and tea were the main liquids consumed. Things that tasted good and didn't require a lot of skill or time to prepare were no doubt favorites. Each man took his turn at "cook week", and was allowed to have his wife accompany him and assist him during that week. Rebecca Ryder said that when a man's turn came to cook, he did so whether he knew how or not! They must have learned fast. There was no mechanical refrigeration, but since the station was only fully manned in the colder months it would not be too difficult to keep food outdoors or in the unheated boat room. Many of our family's favorite non-meat recipes call for molasses, sugar, flour, water, spices, evaporated milk and eggs. All of these items required little refrigeration. When photographs of Life Saving crews are carefully examined, it can be seen that the men appear to be in excellent physical condition. The only man who showed a tendency to be portly is the Keeper. He did not routinely walk the beach patrol, but probably ate just as much as his men. In all of the factual and fictional articles that I've read about Cape Cod Life Saving stations there has never been any mention made of bad or inadequate food. No doubt many of these men never had eaten so well, or at least were very appreciative of what they ate. By looking at the wide array of kitchen utensils and pans provided, one can see that there was no limit to what could have been cooked in the Old Harbor Station kitchen. One thing that does not appear on the list is a can opener!

STOVE, COOKING, BEAVER RANGE - A coal burning cookstove received in April of 1898. Made by the Danville Stove & Mfg. Co., Danville, Pa. It was replaced with a Crawford range in 1904.

HARD COAL, SOFT COAL, OR WOOD
SIX HOLES

The Station received an average of 19 ³/₄ tons of coal a year from 1898 to 1922. Usage during the period 1898 to 1910 was 15.87 tons a year. During this time, there was one Beaver or Crawford kitchen range and three Princess Beaver heaters to supply with coal. After the central heating system was installed in 1910, usage went to an average of nearly 24 tons a year! The coal was purchased from Nickerson Lumber Co., A.C. Ellis, or William Snow. Some of the coal is described as egg size, some as furnace coal, and some as stove coal. In the early years, it was probably transported by horse and wagon down the beach to the station. Later, at least some of it was brought in coal bags across the harbor by dory. There is also some evidence that two dories were lashed together and an early truck positioned on top of them, then floated across the harbor! The dories were loaded at the foot of Bar Cliff Avenue or the Cow Yard (off Old Harbor Road), rowed across, and the coal was carried up the beach to the station. This work is known to have been contracted out to local men by Oscar Nickerson of Nickerson Lumber.

THE HUB HEATER

Hub Coal Heater – used in the Messroom, Keeper's Quarters, and the Bunkroom

The Messroom

The messroom was the large room located on the Southeast corner of the main building. Access to the room was either through the adjacent kitchen, the front piazza, or the boatroom. The messroom was furnished with a large dining table with extension leaves, a Princess Beaver coal stove, a mantel, bookshelves, enough wooden chairs to seat the crew and occasional guests, and a kerosene table lamp for light. The table was covered with an oilcloth of unknown color. This was where the men ate, talked, smoked cigars and pipes, played cards, read the paper, and studied various instruction books provided. The messroom could be considered the heart and nerve center of the station. While Keeper Hezekiah Doane was in charge, grace was said at the table before each meal. "Heavenly Father, bestow Thy blessing. Make us truly thankful. Pardon our sins.

24

Amen." Meals were served at 7 am, noon and 4 pm. No doubt the men coming off watch at 8 pm drank coffee or tea to warm themselves. They may have eaten "duty food" at this time as well. Duty food was that which was their duty to eat, no matter how old.

The following is quoted from a *Harpers Monthly* selection,
"Life-Savers on Old Malabar":

"The eight husky men were sitting not too far from the kitchen stove, puffing on pipes of corn-cob and brier, filling the room with strong tobacco smoke and deliberate conversation. Not one of them seemed over one hundred and sixty pounds, but they were of the sort of stuff that would make any rowing coach's heart hunger to train – clear skinned, deep-chested men, quick and well balanced, of medium size, but tough as whalebone, bright eyed and alert; the product of careful selection trained to the minute by right living, good feeding, and lively work in the brisk air."

Drawing by Harold M. Brett, from Life-Savers on Old Malabar, Harper's Monthly, 1907

OFF DUTY—A GAME OF "63"

Surfmen engaged in a game of "63" at Monomoy Point Station

The Tower, Workshop, Stable, Paint, Phones and Lighting

The Tower - A four-story hipped-roof lookout tower, with the top floor somewhat larger, was situated between the two sections of the Station on the ocean side. The interior of the tower watch room measured approximately 10 $^1/_2$ feet square. The watch room floor had a trap door, which was normally kept closed to allow

for a smooth surface to stand on. There were two windows on each face of the tower, which could be opened for ventilation or an unobstructed view when using the telescope.

Initially, there was no provision for heat in the tower, but when central heat was installed in 1910, a radiator was located there. The man on watch could not leave, even to eat, unless properly relieved. Normally, watches were stood in the tower only during clear weather and daylight hours. The man on duty recorded weather conditions, ships sighted, and any other information the Keeper wanted, in the so-called "Rough Log". From this the Keeper could prepare his daily journal, and weekly transcript for mailing to the District Superintendent. The important items of equipment that were in the tower included the telescope, a pair of binoculars, a Seth Thomas clock, and a thermometer. Some stations had a barometer in the tower but the Inventory Log of Old Harbor Station shows only one having been received, and it was probably kept in the

messroom. There it would be accessible to the crew and the Keeper. In 1918, a speaking tube was installed in the tower and led down to the messroom. This enabled the man on watch to talk to another crewman on the main floor. There were no chairs, books, reading materials, etc. allowed in the lookout tower. Richard A. Ryder told me, however, that he had seen Keeper Doane leading his crew in hymn singing in the tower on Sunday mornings!

The Workshop - When the station was first built, the various tools that were on hand must have been stored in an outbuilding, as the cellar was not dug until October 1900. Since the crew accomplished all maintenance of the building, there was a very extensive collection of hand tools and supplies available for use. Replacing broken window panes and screens, painting, doing minor boat repairs, soldering, rope splicing and carpentry were well within the capabilities of the Keeper or his men. A second shop building measuring 18' x 30', was finished in October 1906. It was finished 38 days after receipt of the building materials, so the Keeper probably built it during the slack summer season. It was located to the South of the main building. This shop remained at the site after the main building was moved to Provincetown in 1977, but was later moved adjacent to the boathouse ¹/₂ mile away. It was destroyed in the "Perfect Storm" in October 1991.

The Stable - The stable was separate from the main building for obvious reasons. A stable was on the beach prior to Old Harbor Station being built, as it was left there when Chatham Station was moved back to the mainland. From 1898 until 1905, the Government is reported to have rented a horse during the winter. The horse was very important to the men, as they would have to pull the apparatus cart and the boat wagon by themselves if there was no horse. Also, the horse was a means of transportation off the beach if the water was too rough to row across to town. A new stable was built in August 1902. The first government owned horse, a bay, arrived in October 1905. It was replaced with a 1300 lb. black horse in January 1909. This horse lived until September 17th, 1916, when it was shot by order of the District Superintendent. A sorrel horse with four white feet arrived on October 5th, 1916. The following day, medicine for the horse was purchased from L. S. Atwood of Chatham for 75 cents. This medicine consisted of one package of Hess Stock Tonic, one package of bran, and one package of dry ginger.

It is not known how long this horse lived, but a Fordson-Trackson tractor arrived in 1922, and an Allis-Chalmers tractor with caterpillar treads and a beach apparatus trailer replaced the Fordson in 1933. On occasion, the crew gathered firewood from along the high tide line, using this tractor and trailer. During the years from 1906 to 1922, the station horse consumed an average of l04 bushels of oats and 2.4 tons of hay a year. The oats and hay were usually purchased from Oscar C. Nickerson (Nickerson Lumber Co.) in Chatham or the Young Brothers in East Harwich. Horseshoeing was carried out several times a year by A. J. Fulcher in Orleans.

Paint - Painting must have taken up any time the crew had left after completing their drills, patrols, etc. Regulations required specific colors of paint on certain surfaces, at prescribed intervals. Boats needed to be painted and varnished, interior surfaces needed attention, and the paints initially had to be made at the scene from raw ingredients received. Later on, premixed paint was received, but it still had to be made ready (stirred a lot) before application.

Phones - All Life Saving Stations on the East side of Cape Cod were linked together by U.S. Government telephone service well before Old Harbor Station was built. Actual connection to this system was made on January 18, 1899. There were phones in the halfway houses at the ends of the patrols so the surfman could readily get in contact with the station in case a wreck was discovered. The Coast Guard maintained the poles and lines until the 1950s, when they were removed.

A Milburn Light

Lighting – Until 1933, all of the lighting in Old Harbor Station was provided by lamps and lanterns that burned kerosene. In that year, a generator-powered 32-volt electric light system was installed.

Unusual emergency type lighting was the Milburn Light, which was received in 1908. It burned acetylene gas, which was produced by combining calcium carbide and water in a lower tank unit. The Milburn light was not often used, but would have proved invaluable in illuminating the scene of a wreck. The light produced was rated at 1000 candlepower.

CHAPTER 5

The Early Years at Old Harbor - 1898 to 1915

*The following entries were extracted from the
Annual Reports of the U.S. Life Saving Service,
the original Station Logbook, and local newspapers*

1897 - Tuesday, August 31 - "The new Life-Saving Station on North Beach is in course of construction. There are several applicants for the position of Keeper." (From the *Chatham Monitor*)

1898 - February 22 - "The Life-Saving Station at North Chatham has been accepted by the Government. Frank Gifford will be the watchman until the station is occupied by the crew." (*Chatham Monitor*)

1898 - March 1 - "Captain Hezekiah Doane assumed his duties as Keeper of Old Harbor Station on Tuesday morning. It is expected that supplies will arrive soon and the station will be manned by a full crew before long." (*Chatham Monitor*) Captain Doane had to go to the Customs House at Barnstable to take his oath of office for keepership.

Keeper Hezekiah F. Doane, age 56
Photograph from *The Life Savers of Cape Cod* by J. W. Dalton

1898 - March 22 - Keeper Doane met Superintendent Sparrow at Harwichport to contract for surfboats for Old Harbor Station. The boats were to be built by Mr. Charles Jenkins of that town.

1898 - May 1st - Station officially manned by Keeper Hezekiah Doane and six surfmen. The men were Robert F. Pierce, #1 man; James E. Jones, #2; Edwin P. Ellis, #3; George F. Kenrick, #4; Benjamin O. Eldredge, #5; and Rufus A. Nickerson, #6. (Nickerson was transferred on August 17th, 1898 and replaced by Otis C. Eldredge.)

1898 – May 7 - Received one Monomoy surfboat, without centerboard, 24/8" long x 6/6" beam, built by Charles Jenkins in Harwichport.

1898 - May 24 - The first recorded instance of help rendered by the crew of Old Harbor Station. The American fishing schooner *LORNA DOONE* mistook lights on shore and stranded on Chatham bar shortly after mid-night. The station crew boarded her, followed shortly by the Chatham Station crew and a crew from shore. The schooner's crew was unharmed. The master made a contract with the men from shore to float the vessel. The Old Harbor crew took a telegram ashore for the owners, and later in the day carried one off to the master from the owners. The contractors released the vessel on the 25th, apparently undamaged.

1898 - May 30 - Seeing a vessel out of the regular track, Surfman Pierce on patrol burned a hand-held Coston signal and the vessel altered her course.

1898 - May 31- An unnamed yacht parted her moorings and was drift-ing to sea. The surfmen went out in a dory and took her to a safe berth.

1898 - June 23 - Received one Monomoy surfboat, with centerboard; same dimensions and builder as the one received on May 7th.

1898 - August 17 - An unnamed small boat became unmanageable in a strong wind, owing to the inexperience of its occupant. Surfmen from the station went out to her in a dory and took her back to town.

1898 - August 19 - The crew was employed erecting a drill pole.

1898 - August 25 - When the crew drilled with the beach apparatus, the time from the order "Action" to landing the #6 man at the wooden crotch supporting the breeches buoy hawser was 4 $\frac{1}{2}$ minutes. The distance from crotch to pole was 55 yards.

1898 - August 27 - A dory anchored in the channel, its occupants (two women and a man) having become tired out by rowing against a strong current. When they tried to get their anchor, they found that it was fouled on a piece of sunken wreckage and could not be raised. Surfmen Pierce and Eldredge went off to them in a dory, cleared their anchor, and saw them safely to the landing.

1898 - August 31- The catboat *COSMOS*, Captain William Smith, had her halyards carried away while beating into Chatham Inlet. Her crew anchored and set a distress signal. Two surfmen went off to her in a dory, assisted in reeving the halyards, and sailing her to her moorings in the harbor.

1898 - September 17 - Two men in the small catboat *ETTA* anchored off the station, having been prevented from entering Chatham Harbor by the heavy surf on the bar. The station crew boarded the craft and brought the men to the station, where they remained overnight.

1898 - November 14 - The catboat *CHARLIE C.*, Captain Nickerson, in attempting one of the side channels into Chatham, stranded on the bar. Owing to a falling tide nothing could be done until the next flood. At that time, the station crew kedged her into deep water and piloted her into the main channel, from which place the master took her into the harbor.

1898 - November 29 - Bodies of five people who perished in the great storm (the *PORTLAND* gale) were washed upon the beach between this date and December 1. Surfmen took charge of them until removed by the proper local authorities.

The *City of Portland*, courtesy of the Maine Historical Society

The following are comments made to noted maritime historian Edward Rowe Snow by former Old Harbor Station Surfman Benjamin O. Eldredge:

"I was at the Old Harbor Station on the Saturday after Thanksgiving that year. I was outside the station washing my whites and soon became a little apprehensive because of the atmospheric conditions. I looked across the Bay and there was a queer blue light over everything. All around the station the surfmen were in a similar mood, not joking as they usually do, but strangely silent. The gulls were screaming and calling out raucously. We knew something was going to happen. My watch started at four o'clock and ended at eight. It is usually called the sunset watch. The weather was pretty good, but a stiff breeze began to blow. Then came Sunday, November 27. My partner began his patrol at four o'clock in the morning, but didn't get back until ten. By then it was blowing very hard. A short time later all quieted down, and we realized we were in the eye of the hurricane. Then it began to blow again, worse than before. The sea and the tide came rushing in through the hollows. This created narrow ridges with the ocean on the outside so close to the inside beach that I could have thrown a stone from one side to the other. It was a terrible night, but Monday morning eventually arrived. I was up in the cupola of the station scanning the beach with my spyglass, known today as a telescope. I noticed something, apparently a log, but wishing to be certain, launched a dory and rowed down to where the object was. I will never forget the first body we found from the Steamer *PORTLAND*. It was the body of a woman, Mrs. Cordelia Mitchell who, we found out later, had spent Thanksgiving with her son in Braintree. She was naked except for shoes, stockings, and garters. It was a terrible week that we spent. Sometimes we could see just a hand sticking up in the sand, and when we dug, of course, we exposed a body. I remember Captain Elbert Williams, a fisherman from Boothbay Harbor. Not only did he have all his clothes on, but also he had wrapped a comforter tightly around his head. One man came in with his pockets filled with lead pencils. Another one was a discharged Spanish-American War veteran. You might expect to find his watch and chain in his vest pocket, but we took them out of his pants. One man came up on shore December 5 with his pockets and sleeves so full of sand he must have rolled along the bottom of the shore. He could not have floated. Altogether we discovered nine bodies, with one pair being a bride and groom. Over at the Orleans Station they also found nine bodies."

Mr. Eldredge and Mr. Snow were convinced that the *PORTLAND* had met its doom in a collision with either the *ADDIE E. SNOW* or the *PENTAGOET*.

"I remember the *(EDITH) NUTE*, the *HORATIO HALL* and the *J. H. DIMMOCK*. The last two collided with each other."

(These wrecks occurred in later years near the Old Harbor Station. Mr. Eldredge ultimately became President of the Cape Cod Five Cents Savings Bank.)

1898 - December 5 - The station lookout found a man's body on the beach near the station. Surfmen took it to North Chatham in a dory and delivered it to the coroner.

1898 - December 6 - Two surfmen picked up the body of a colored man on the beach two miles north of the station. It was delivered to the proper authorities.

1898 - December 7 - During the first watch the patrol fired a Coston signal to warn a schooner that was nearly on the bar, and she immediately stood out into deeper water.

1899 - February 13 - "The high tides and heavy cakes of ice running through the cuts in the beach between this and Orleans stations will make it impossible for the 8 to midnight patrols to meet. Very dangerous patrolling in the N.E. blizzard which prevails to night (sic). H. F. Doane, Keeper" (As written in the Old Harbor Station log.)

1899 - February 14 - "Crew employed shoveling snow from the building."

1899 - February 19 - At 7 pm the south patrol saw a schooner dangerously near the beach. He burned a Coston signal, which caused her to keep away and go clear.

1899 - March 25 - The south patrolman, (substitute Dean N. Eldridge), saw a schooner in danger of stranding on the bar and warned her off by burning a Coston signal.

Firing a Coston Signal

1899 - March 31 - The surfman on north patrol burned a Coston signal and warned a schooner off a dangerous course.

1899 - May 10 - During the first watch Surfman Kenrick, on patrol, warned a schooner off the beach.

1899 - August 21 - The sloop yacht *THEA* stranded 1 1/2 miles south of the station while trying to enter the harbor during threatening weather, with a pleasure party of four persons on board. The lifesaving crew boarded her in a surfboat, carried out her anchor, and, after the tide began to flood, succeeded in hauling her afloat, apparently undamaged. They took her to a safe anchorage within Chatham Harbor.

Drawing by Chatham artist Harold M. Brett, from *Life-Savers on Old Malabar*, from *Harper's Monthly*, 1907

1899 - August 25 - After a party of men and women landed in three small skiffs to visit the station, the sea became too rough for them to return to Chatham in their small boats. The lifesaving crew launched the surfboat and transported them safely back to town.

1899 - October 19 - Practiced using the life car. The surfboat was anchored offshore and the shot line was fired over it. The hawser was then made fast to the surfboat and the life car employed.

1899 - October 23 - The American schooner *JENNY GREENBANK* was discovered by the station patrol, Oliver E. Eldredge, aground on Chatham Bar at 2:00 am. The station crew reached her in the surfboat at 2:45 am, and soon succeeded in hauling her afloat, but, as she was inside other shoals, she stranded again. They then threw some of her cargo of coal overboard, but failed to release her, the tide having begun to ebb. At daylight a salvage crew came off from Chatham, with whom the master made a bargain to float his vessel. Surfmen transported the master to and from the shore, in order that he might communicate with his owners. The schooner was floated upon the next high water without apparent injury, and proceeded to her destination.

1899 - November 7 - During a routine surfboat drill, the time from the command "Unload" to "Ready for Launching" was logged at 40 seconds.

1899 - November 14 - An unnamed fishing boat stranded on one of the shoals while coming in from the fishing grounds. Three of the station crew went out in the dory and helped float the boat.

1899 - November 16 - The hired horse went on duty. He was to stay until March 31st, 1900.

1900 - January 23 - A three masted schooner was warned off the beach by the south patrol.

1900 – January 27 – "The terrific northwest gale, the heaviest blow for nearly a year, came very near claiming the lives of five Rockland seamen today, whose vessel the schooner *HELEN*, Capt. Hutchins, after losing both her fore and main sail through their catching fire from the burning cargo of lime, began to drift seaward. Fortunately a friendly tug was near, and with the assistance of the life-saving crews of the Orleans and Old Harbor Stations the five men were taken off, all badly frost bitten, while the schooner also was saved. The crew had a terrible experience yesterday afternoon, last night, and this fore-noon battling with the fire and the mighty seas that were breaking over the little schooner, threatened with the great accumulation of ice to sink her". (*From the* New York Times, *January 28th, 1900.*)

1900 - March 17 - Received one 22 foot Monomoy surfboat, with spars, sails, and rudder. The existing 24 foot surfboat without a centerboard was to be delivered in trade to Jenkins, the builder. Both surfboats at the station were now of the sailing type, with centerboards.

1900 - August 1 - The surfmen at the station as of this date were Robert F. Pierce, Edwin P. Ellis, George F. Kenrick, Benjamin O. Eldredge, Otis C. Eldredge, and Albert F. Long.

1900 - September 11 - An unnamed fishing boat broke adrift from moorings in Chatham Roads. Surfmen pulled out and overhauled the boat, sailed it to a safe anchorage, and notified the owner of its whereabouts.

1900 - October 22 - Completed one boathouse and dug one small cellar (nine feet square) under the main building.

1901 - July 23 - A new telephone cable was laid across the inlet between Old Harbor and Chatham stations. The old cable had been inoperative since April.

Open House at Old Harbor Lifesaving Station, August 1901.
Photo taken from the "Wreck Pole", the pole used by the surfmen
to practice the weekly Beach Apparatus Drill.

1901 - August 21 - The crew put on a public demonstration of the beach apparatus and surfboat, as well as signal and resuscitation drills. There were 400 people in attendance!

1901 - August 29 - An unnamed sailboat accidentally stranded. The man in charge came to the station for help, and surfmen assisted him to get his boat afloat and make sail, when he proceeded on his way.

1901 - October 17 - The American schooner *FRANCES M*, of Bath, Me. with her head gear all carried away, made an anchorage about four miles east of the station. She had collided with the schooner *CLARA GOODWIN* about ten miles offshore. Surfmen boarded her and assisted to clear away the wreckage, which was hanging under her bow; then, the wind being fair, the master sailed to Boston for repairs.

1902 - January 8 - Captain Doane and crew brought ashore the crew of the schooner *COMMERCE*, which was blown to sea. The schooner crew had initially been picked up by the tug *LACKAWANNA*. Captain Pearson of the *COMMERCE* abandoned the vessel when he found it was being driven to sea.

1902 - February 13 - The fishing schooner *ELSIE M. SMITH*, of 112 tons burden, hailing from Gloucester, Massachusetts, and carrying eighteen men, all told, sailed on February 10, 1902, for the fishing grounds some twenty miles off the elbow of Cape Cod. At about 9:30 in the night of the 13th, she stranded on Orleans Beach and became a total wreck, involving the loss of two lives, needlessly sacrificed in the attempt made by three of the crew to reach land in one of the dories. The schooner arrived on the fishing grounds the day after leaving Gloucester, and during the following 48 hours succeeded in taking on board a catch of 10,000 pounds; but on the 13th, the sea was so rough that fishing became impracticable, and she was compelled to stand off and on, and at times heave to. After darkness shut down, the wind came on heavy from the NE, with frequent snow squalls and almost continuous thick weather. The captain, who was among the rescued, stated that he had given instructions to tack ship by 9 pm, but that the land not being visible he had no idea of his proximity to it, and at five minutes past nine the vessel struck the outer bar. He at once attempted to swing her off by easing the main sheet, but she would not mind the helm, and a few moments later fetched up on the inner bar, where she soon pounded her seams open and filled.

Most of the crew took to the rigging for temporary safety, but a portion of them seemed to be panic-stricken, and apparently thought of nothing but an effort to reach the shore at once in their dories, although the sea was very rough and the surf running far too high for such a venture. Nevertheless, with headlong haste, in total disregard of the instructions of the master, a dory was pushed overboard and got away, fortunately without anybody in it. A second one was then launched and smashed to pieces alongside; but, still unheeding, the desperate men shoved a third one overboard and two of them clambered in. Scarcely had it passed twenty feet from the vessel when it capsized and threw the men into the water. Happily, both of them were swept to the beach by the rushing seas, and thus their lives were saved in spite of their folly. The remainder of those who had resolved to quit the schooner at all hazards still took no warning, and, without waiting to find out what had become of those who had already left, plunged another dory over the rail and three of them jumped into it. Hardly had they got their oars into the rowlocks when a great comber caught up the craft and hurled it end over end, pitching the occupants into the sea. They could not return to the vessel, and simply had to do their best to keep afloat and gain the shore - a desperate chance, which only one succeeded in making good. The other two, Dean and Silvina Daucett, brothers, hailing from Yarmouth, Nova Scotia, were not able to contend successfully with the terrible odds, and in a few moments disappeared.

Elsie M. Smith ashore

The place on the beach where the vessel stranded was about three miles NNE of the Old Harbor Station and about two miles S¹/₂ E of the Orleans Station. When she struck, Surfmen D. N. Eldridge, of the former, and M. K. Young, of the latter, were at the halfway house. While they were traveling their beats, the schooner was so far offshore, burning no signal, and the snow was falling so thick that neither of them saw any sign of her; but as soon as she struck the inner bar Eldridge caught a glimpse of her port light. Young had carefully scanned the sea only a moment or two earlier, so that it is probable Eldridge discovered her the very instant she stranded - about 9:20 pm. He promptly burned a red Coston light, and while it was still flaming, Young ran into the halfway house and called the Orleans station over the telephone. Then, leaving Eldridge to call up the Old Harbor station, he ran down to the beach opposite the wreck, which was about a third of a mile to the northward, meeting on his way the two men who first left the schooner and were cast ashore. He directed them to the halfway house for shelter. As soon as he arrived abreast of the wreck he went close down to the surf as the waves receded and shouted to those on board that assistance would soon be at hand, and they should by all means make no effort to land by themselves. The vessel was at this time about 150 yards distant. Eldridge stated to each Keeper, by telephone, the nature and position of the wreck, and then proceeded to join Young, who remained on the beach with his lantern doing what he could to encourage the men on the wreck. On his way Eldridge conversed with the two fishermen already referred to, who told him that three others had left the schooner in another dory, but were probably lost. Nevertheless, he turned to the south'ard and patrolled the beach for half a mile with the hope of finding them.

Seeing nothing, he returned and joined Young. Both men now remained where they were until the arrival of their comrades. Keeper Doane appeared with the Old Harbor crew at about 10 pm, and Keeper Charles arrived with the Orleans crew a few minutes later. Two men were promptly sent off to patrol the shore, while the rest got to work to set up the beach apparatus and put it in operation. It was then the first of the flood tide with a very strong undertow running to the south, and the seas were breaking all over the wreck, which was rolling and pounding savagely, with her foresail and head sails still set, and her mainsail only halfway down. Haste was necessary. The Lyle gun was swiftly placed in position, and the first shot carried the line fairly across the jib stay. The fishermen reached it without great difficulty, and quickly hauled it in with the whip line attached, but when they got the hawser which was bent to the whip line, they were slow - more than half an hour - in making it fast, a fact which they afterwards explained was due to their numbed condition and to the necessity for clearing several turns in the whip line. It appears also that they spent some time in trying to attach the hawser to the fore-mast, which was desirable, but proved impossible, and therefore it was bent to the foreshrouds. The sand anchor had already been planted, but the rush of the incoming tide and current drove the wreck southward, and the anchor had to be moved also in that direction. Probably these operations consumed something like an hour, which was actually very good time. In the meantime, the third man cast ashore from the wreck appeared on shore and was sent to the halfway house. When the hawser was finally made fast on board the ship, and the shore end set up, the breeches buoy was put in place and sent out. There were thirteen to come ashore, and they came one by one, the life-savers running far into the surf to hold them up and aid them. The last man was landed at 12:20 am. There were in all sixteen of them, and they were equally divided between the two stations, where they were taken as soon as possible and supplied dry clothing from the supply furnished by the Women's National Relief Association, given a good warm meal, and otherwise made comfortable.

The next day all except the captain were sent to Boston, free transportation having been furnished them. It was 2:10 in the morning when the Old Harbor crew returned to their station, and 2:40 when the Orleans crew reached theirs. The bodies of the two men who drowned were subsequently found in the vicinity and reverently buried in the cemetery at Chatham. Had the entire crew patiently remained on board the schooner until arrival of the lifesavers, none would have been lost. On the other hand, had there been no lifesaving stations in the vicinity, all (as they themselves testified), must have frozen to death in the rigging, or, if they had drifted ashore, miserably perished on the bleak, mid-winter sands.

The following narrative by former Surfman Benjamin O. Eldredge is excerpted from the Cape Cod Compass, *1963:*

"One of the worst nights I ever remember was the 15th of February on a Saturday night with a wild nor'east storm of gale winds and heavy snow. My partner and I started off on our patrol from eight to twelve midnight. Just as I reached the 'half-way house,' I could hear that new-fangled telephone they'd just installed and I knew something was up! I listened in and sure enough it was my partner telling the Captain way back at the Station that he had spotted a ship driven in on the bars about half-way to Orleans. I really plowed back up that beach in record

Typical Cape Cod "half-way house", courtesy of the Chatham Historical (MA) Society

time paying no mind to that blizzard ... I was so determined to get there in time to show the older men how fast and strong I was. Somehow I made it and got there just as the Orleans crew arrived with all their equipment. That was one of the times when the crew had to cover the heads of the horses that pulled the surfboat and breeches-buoy gear and cannon; even those trained horses wouldn't have that wind-driven sand and snow without protection. She [the *ELSIE M. SMITH*] had beached fast out there and in that raging wind and driving snow it was about the hardest job we ever had to get a line aboard her; we couldn't even see her half the time. The tide had already started turning and there was danger she might be washed back where we couldn't hold her to man the breeches-buoy. When we were hauling in one of the men from the ship we nearly lost him. There was such an undertow that our 'weather-whip' got caught shoreside of the buoy and it was almost impossible to rescue him. Afterwards we had to put two men on that line to handle it - I'd never seen that done before! I can tell you there wasn't much skin left on our hands after that night's work! We didn't have the heavy cotton gloves that the seamen use now - and the 'Nova Scotia Mittens' we used were not much good for this kind of work. The mittens were made of wool and shrank up tight in the salt water - and they were soon pulled off, what with hauling back and forth on a wet, sandy rope."

Cape Cod National Seashore oral history file.

1902 - February 23 - The patrol picked up the body of a man on Chatham beach, which was thought to be that of one of the two men lost in the surf while attempting to land in a dory from the wrecked schooner *ELSIE M. SMITH* on February 13. Men of the Chatham station picked the other man's body up the same day.

1902 - March 22 - The sloop *LARK* capsized at 8:30 am, during a strong wind, a half-mile NW of the station. Her occupants, two men, were clinging to the bottom of the sloop. The Keeper, with his own fifteen-foot dory manned by two surfmen, went to the place, rescued the men, righted the sloop, and towed her into shoal water.

1902 - May 21 - The 30 foot racing sloop *WILLIWIN* from Boston anchored off the station and communicated to the Keeper that he wished to enter Chatham Harbor. Surfmen pulled off to her, made sail, and took her to a snug berth inside.

1902 - May 30 - The yacht *MARGUERITE* from Hartford, Ct. anchored three miles SE of the station during a heavy westerly gale, and was dragging offshore. In response to the distress signal, which her master displayed, the Keeper hitched the horse to the boat wagon and transported the surfboat to a point $^3/_4$ of a mile to the south'ard of the yawl, where the surf was sufficiently smooth to enable him to launch. Surfmen found four men, inexperienced in yacht sailing, on board of her, and immediately started to heave up her anchors. After four hours of hard labor they succeeded in working her to a safe berth under the beach off Chatham. When the wind moderated later in the day, they took her into Chatham Harbor. Her crew left for their homes by train. At the request of her owner, the Keeper engaged men to sail her to her destination.

1902 - August - A new stable for the rented horse was completed.

1902 – August 6 - The sloop *SACHEM* stranded at 12:30 pm, a half mile from the station, while entering harbor for shelter from bad weather. Surfmen boarded in the surfboat, ran anchors, and at high water hove the vessel afloat uninjured, and took her to a safe berth.

1902 - August 9 - In response to a signal from the American schooner *INTREPID*, the life-saving crew boarded the schooner, at anchor 1 $^1/_2$ miles SE from the station, and the Keeper piloted her over Chatham Bar and into Orleans Bay.

1902 - August 17 - A small skiff was drifting rapidly out of the harbor, carrying a small boy who was helpless. Surfmen rescued the lad and towed the boat ashore.

1902 - August 26 - A waterlogged and unattended dory was drifting down the tide. Surfmen secured the boat and returned it to the owner.

1902 - September 1 - A sloop carried away her mast during a regatta, and was towed to an anchorage by the station crew, who were in attendance to render aid in case of necessity.

1903 - April 11- The American sloop *MAGGIE CANNON* sprung her mast in a strong breeze while enroute from Boston to New London, and lay to off the bar two miles ESE of the station, displaying a signal of distress. The lookout sighted her at 5 pm, and the station crew went to her aid in the small surfboat. Finding her short of provisions and unable to make port, they took a line from her bow and towed her with the surfboat into Chatham Harbor for repairs and supplies. On the morning of the 13th she started out the channel, but grounded, and the surfmen assisted her afloat and piloted her to sea.

1903 - August 1st - The surfmen at the station as of this date were Robert F. Pierce, Edwin P. Ellis, Benjamin O. Eldredge, Otis C. Eldredge, Dean N. Eldridge, and Francis H. Bassett.

1903 - August 24 - Surfmen towed an unattended drifting rowboat to the station, where it was held to await the owner.

1903 - August 29 - The steam launch *MONOMOY* parted her moorings in a fresh NE wind and rough sea and stranded 1 1/2 miles SSW of the station at 5 am. The lookout promptly reported the casualty and the life saving crew pulled to her, ran anchors, hove her afloat, and towed her into Chatham Harbor with the surfboat.

1903 - September 9 - The wind breezed up and made it dangerous for a party of nine persons in a dory to recross the harbor, so they were taken in the surfboat and safely landed.

1903 - October 22 - Received one eighteen-foot Swampscott model surf dory and equipment. The dory cost $35.00.

1904 - April 29 - During a thick fog the American schooner *FUTURE* stranded on Nauset Beach, 3/4 mile NNE of the station. The heavy surf making it impossible to launch the surfboat, the lifesavers immediately started to her assistance with the beach apparatus. After a hard drag through the soft sand, the apparatus was set up abreast of the schooner, a line was fired across her, and the crew of eight men were landed in the breeches buoy. The rescued men were taken to the station, furnished with dry clothing, and succored at the station for 48 hours. The vessel was floated on May 6, after which the salvage crew was landed by the lifesavers.

1904 - May 27 - The lookout having reported the sloop *BETTY* of Boston as flying a signal of distress, the life-saving crew launched the surfboat, went to her, and found that she was leaking and that the master, who had severely strained himself while endeavoring to heave up her anchor, was unable to get the vessel underway. The surfmen made sail on her, got her underway, and brought her into Chatham Harbor.

1904 - July 1 - About midnight, in a thick fog, the British barkentine *ALBERTINA* collided with an obstruction in Pollock Rip Slue, staving a large hole in her bow, and was making water fast. To save her from sinking the master ran her aground on Chatham Bar, two miles south of the station.

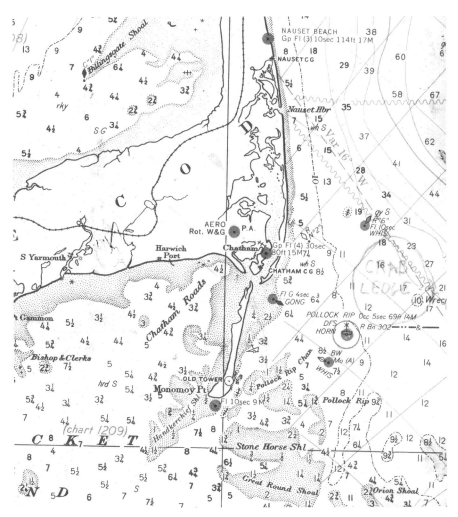

Nautical Chart showing Pollock Rip, the "Crab Ledge" fishing ground and adjacent shoals. (Soundings in feet at low water)

At 7 am the Keeper sighted her upper spars over the fog bank, and immediately mustered a temporary crew (it was the inactive season), and put out to her in the surfboat. A salvage crew also boarded the vessel, but nothing could be done for her relief at the time; after arranging with the master to communicate by signal in case of need, the Keeper returned to the station and dismissed his crew. Three days later, in response to a signal, the Keeper, with Keeper Eldridge of the Chatham Lifesaving station, again mustered a crew, went to the barkentine, and brought on shore the wife of the master and a quantity of personal effects. The following day a Board of Survey condemned the vessel and she was stripped and abandoned. The wreck was considered a hazard to navigation and subsequently dynamited by the War Department Engineers.

Vessel Albertina *being stripped after being abandoned.*
Men are tricing up sails, etc. for offloading.
Photo taken from a dory by Henry Pennypacker.

1904 - September 3 - The British schooner *CORA MAY* stranded on Chatham Bar two miles south of Chatham station at 8 pm, during a thick fog, wind moderate, sea rough. At 9 pm the north patrol from Chatham station heard her foghorn and caught a glimpse of her lights, and telephoned the station. The Keeper in turn telephoned to Old Harbor station, and the life-saving crews made vigilant search during the night. They were unsuccessful owing to the fact that a party of wreckers had found the schooner, after which her foghorn ceased blowing, and her lights were extinguished. In the morning, both crews reached the stranded craft. Finding it impossible to get her afloat on account of the state of sea and weather, and her position being one of danger, the crew were taken to the Old Harbor station and succored there for the night. In the morning her crew and the lifesavers returned to the vessel, which floated as the tide came in, and Keeper Doane piloted her to a safe anchorage. She was found to have sustained only slight injury, and later in the day proceeded on her voyage.

1904 - September 8 - Beach apparatus drill time, from the order "Action" to landing the #6 man at the crotch, had been reduced to 2 minutes, 35 seconds.

1904 - October 13 - The British schooner *WENTWORTH* stranded on Chatham Bar and all hands perished. She had sailed from Nova Scotia on October 11, bound for Newark, N.J., with a cargo of plaster and a crew of seven. The master owned one-quarter interest in her, and was accompanied on the voyage by his wife and three small children. Surfman Bassett first discovered the vessel at 7:20 pm on the south patrol. The weather was squally, with occasional light drizzle. It had been blowing hard all day from the northeast, making up an unusually heavy sea by nightfall. The surfman had reached the end of his beat and was about to retrace his steps when the faint sound of a foghorn reached him. He at once called up the Keeper on the phone and informed him that he could hear a horn, probably from a vessel in trouble off the bar. He ran down to the surf, where he could barely make out the outlines of a schooner. He at once burned a Coston signal to inform the crew of the schooner that their situation had been observed and that help was at hand. He then hastily returned to the station to report the stranded craft and assist the life-saving crew with the beach apparatus. Upon receipt of the phone message from the patrol, the Keeper went up into the look-out tower, from which point he could make out a dark object to the south'ard, which he took to be a vessel. He gave the alarm and ordered out the beach apparatus. A Coston signal was burned from the station, but no response came from the schooner. The north patrol not having returned yet, there were but six men, including the Keeper, at the cart, and the haul through the soft sand was slow and difficult.

They reached the scene of the wreck at 8:30 pm, all being more or less tired out by their exertions. The outlines of the hull and spars could barely be made out in the gathering darkness, a dim light burned in the cabin window, and the flapping sails could be heard above the roar of the surf; but on board no signs of life were apparent and no signals of distress were displayed. The beach apparatus was positioned and a shot was fired over her, a #9 shot line and six oz. of powder being used. After this shot, some of the surfmen thought they could hear shouting on the vessel. The megaphone was used to learn if the shot had been success-ful, but no reply came from the vessel. The jerking of the shot line, how-ever, soon satisfied the Keeper that it had fallen over the vessel and was being hauled aboard. The line was bent on to the whip, which went off rapidly until nearly all of it had run off the reel. Again the megaphone was used to ascertain if the whip block had reached the sailors, but still no response came. Owing to the heavy surf and the strong current, which swept the whip to leeward, the Keeper was unable to tell from the shore whether or not the whip block had reached the vessel, or, if so, whether it had been made fast. After waiting a reasonable time for the whip block to be made fast on board, the hawser was bent on and paid out.

It went off steadily for several yards, but suddenly stopped. The Keeper had the hawser hauled in, whereupon it was discovered that it had become fouled with the whip. Upon hauling in the whip and shot line the offshore end of the latter was found to be fast. No effort had been made by the people on board to haul in the whip line! Whether they had all been washed overboard by the furious sea, which was making a clean breach over the vessel, or driven from the decks for greater safety into the rigging, where they were unable to reach the lifeline could only be surmised. It was certain that they were unable to haul off the whip.

Keeper Doane now took his crew back to the station for the surfboat, leaving his lights still burning on the shore as encouragement to any of the sailors who might yet be on board. The surf was so furious that there was scarcely a prospect that the use of the boat would be possible, but he wished to be ready to make the effort if the opportunity arose. The south patrolman from Orleans station met the Old Harbor crew and helped them get out their surfboat and haul it to the scene. While on the way back, they met three experienced surfmen from town, who had rowed across the harbor and volunteered to assist in hauling the surf-boat. When the party arrived at the wreck scene the surf was even worse than before. The beach apparatus was made ready again, and a second shot fired with six oz. of powder and a #7 line. A Coston signal was burned to attract attention, and the megaphone was again used, but there was no response. After waiting a suitable time for the sailors to get the line, it was hauled in and the shot was found attached, showing that the line had not fallen over the vessel. Just after this shot the cabin lights disappeared and were seen no more. In the meantime Keeper Charles, of the Orleans station, had arrived with his men. They had brought with them a Wells light, which was at once set up, its beams illuminating the shore and sea for a considerable distance. By its light, the vessel, her spars, and hull could be made out with the seas washing over her; but it could not be determined whether she was head or stern on, nor could any signs of life be discovered aboard her. The two Keepers held a conference and studied the situation from every side. Although the surfboat was in readiness, a glance at the sea showed that its use was impossible. It was decided to make another effort to get a line across the vessel, although it was felt to be useless since a line already lay upon her unused. A third shot was fired, a #7 line and a six oz. charge of powder being used, but the result was the same as before - the line did not reach the vessel, and was hauled back to the beach. All that the watchers on shore could do now was to wait for morning and hope the ship held together until then. Patrolmen were dispatched southward to watch for anything that might be washed ashore. The rest of the crew remained opposite the vessel, keeping a fire going and burning frequent signals as encouragement to those who might be on her.

But no sound or signal came from those on board until about 3 am, when a loud crash was heard and fire flashed from her mastheads, as though from the friction of falling wire stays and rigging across each other, indicating that her masts had broken off or fallen, and from over the waters there came a wild shriek of distress - a human cry of despair - the only sound that reached the ears of Keeper Doane that night evidencing that some of the shipwrecked crew were still there. The beach patrol continued their search, but no boats or persons were found, although portions of the vessel's cabin furniture coming ashore showed that she was breaking up. Shortly before daylight the Keeper of the Chatham station reported over the telephone that a name board with *WENTWORTH* on it had been found on the Chatham beach. This was the first knowledge the Old Harbor station crew had of the vessel's name. When day dawned, a dismal picture was revealed. The vessel lay stern on with her hull almost submerged, her bowsprit and jib boom were standing, as was also her foremast. The mainmast was broken off at the deck and hanging by its spring stay against the fore rigging. The mizzenmast lay in the water alongside with a mass of other wreckage, her stern was split open and the after-deck house gone, and the seas washed continually over and through her. No sign of life could be seen anywhere on or around her. At 6 am the patrol saw an object floating near the south point of the beach below the wreck. He waded out and brought ashore the body of a woman. She appeared to be about 25 years of age, was fully clothed, with a blanket loosely knotted around her body, as though it had bound a child to her. The Keeper was notified, and the body was removed to Old Harbor station. A little later the body of a man was picked up on the beach some distance from the wreck. No more bodies were discovered by the patrols. The schooner continued to break up, and at 5 am the following day the foremast fell, carrying with it the bowsprit and jib boom. In the wreckage that washed up, the end of the shot line was found to have been hastily tied to a spoke of the ship's wheel. The body of the captain's wife was shipped to her home. The seaman, Thomas Perguson, was buried in Chatham. The officer who investigated this sad disaster closed his report as follows: "Everything which human power could do was done for the people on this wreck. Had the whole Life-Saving Service been on the scene the result must have been the same."

1904 - November 21 - At 6:30 pm a surfman sighted a lumber-laden schooner dangerously near to Chatham Bar and warned her off with a Coston light.

1904 - November 24 - At 3:30 am the north patrol saw a fishing schooner too close to the beach. He flashed a night signal and she at once stood out for deep water.

1904 - December 1 - Surfman Richard E. Ryder reported for duty as "Winter Man", having been transferred from Gurnet Station, near Plymouth.

1905 - September 2 - The sloop *STOIC* tried to enter Chatham without a pilot and stranded on a shoal two miles south of the station. The station crew went to her assistance in the surfboat, ran out an anchor, floated her when the tide rose, and took her to a good anchorage.

1905 - October 25 - Received the first government-owned horse. Prior to this, a horse was rented for the winter season. (For some reason, there was no horse available for use at the *WENTWORTH* wreck a year earlier.)

1906 - April 18 - As a dory was drifting out of the harbor toward the inlet, several surfmen in a dory pulled out to it and brought it back to the harbor.

1906 - April 20 - The gas launch *TRITON* broke adrift while being towed by a launch. It was recovered by the lifesavers and restored to the owner.

1906 - October 5 - During calms and strong current the catboat *AUK* drifted onto Chatham Bar a quarter mile offshore at 4:40 pm. Upon observing her signal for assistance the surfmen boarded her and carried out anchors, and at flood tide hove her about without damage.

1906 - October 26 - Finished construction of an 18 x 30 foot workshop.

1906 - October 31 - A dory moored a half mile SW from the station capsized in high seas and a strong NNE breeze. Lifesavers went to the boat in the surfboat, righted it and bailed it out, and took it to a safe anchorage.

1906 - December 15 - A boatman in a skiff capsized in a squall and lost his oars. He was towed to his home in North Chatham.

1907 - January 13 - The American steamer *ONONDAGA* stranded at 1:30 am 1 1/2 miles NNE of the station. It was misty weather with a high sea running. Warning was given immediately by the lookout in the tower and the lifesavers proceeded to a point on the beach abreast the vessel. The first shot from the Lyle gun landed the line on her deck and the breeches buoy was sent out to her. As she was in no immediate danger none of her crew were landed. The weather moderated and lifesavers carried out the insurance underwriter and brought dispatches ashore. With the assistance of the towboats *UNDERWRITER* and *STORM KING*, the steamer was floated on March 14th.

Clyde line *SS Onondaga* ashore north of Old Harbor

Old Harbor crew at *Onondaga* scene.
Surfman Ryder is marked by his family with an "X".

1907 - February 3 - Three men who had come over to look at the wrecked steamer *ONONDAGA* were unable to get back, due to a freshening wind. They applied to the life-saving crew for assistance and were taken back to Chatham in the surfboat.

1907 - August 1 - The crew was employed boating hay and grain across the harbor from the Cow Yard to the station.

1907 - August 14 - The gas launch *PALM* anchored two miles south of the station with signals of distress flying. The owner's wife had taken sick, and he wanted to land with his wife and children. The station crew got the *PALM* under way, piloted her into Chatham Harbor, and landed the wife and children. Later, the station crew took the *PALM* out again.

1908 - April 8 - A schooner came dangerously near the beach and was warned off with a Coston signal by the night patrol.

1908 - May 31 - A schooner in danger of standing in too close was warned off with a Coston signal by the night patrol.

1908 - December 22 - The schooner *JULIA A. BERKELE* was discovered at daylight anchored 2 $\frac{1}{2}$ miles SE of the station with a distress signal set in her rigging. The surfboat was manned and the lifesavers went on board. She had been caught out in a squall and her two gaffs and main boom had carried away. The sea was making up and the schooner was in a bad berth, so the surfmen hove up anchor, set her jibs, and stood for Pollock Rip. A signal for aid was hoisted, and the Revenue Cutter *ACUSHNET* came out and towed the schooner to Hyannis.

ACUSHNET

The Revenue Cutter *Acushnet*

1909 - February 27 - Received a drill pole, which replaced the first one. Also referred to as the "Wreck Pole".

1909 - March 9 - The steamer *H. F. DIMOCK* collided with the steamer *HORATIO HALL* and was beached a half mile SSE of Orleans station to avoid sinking. The steamer could not be seen, owing to the dense fog, but her distress signals were heard at the Orleans station. A surfboat was immediately launched and the surfmen went alongside. The master informed the Keeper that the *HORATIO HALL* had sunk, but that he had her passengers and crew aboard. The Keeper took a boatload ashore and telephoned to Nauset and Old Harbor stations for assistance. The work of rescue was continued, and 67 persons were landed. The seas had driven the steamer so close to the shore that it was now within reach of the beach apparatus, so the master and crew remained on board. The town authorities assisted the Keeper in caring for the distressed people, who were hauled in wagons to Orleans and sheltered in hotels and in homes. The next morning the selectmen of Orleans gave the passengers transportation to Boston. On March 11, lifesavers landed baggage and took company officials and underwriters' agents off to the steamer. Four towboats arrived and began salvage operations, floating her on the 14th. On the night of the 13th, the weather became threatening and lifesavers responded to distress whistles of a tug. The surfboat landed 32 salvage workers. The *H. F. DIMOCK* was later towed to Boston.

1909 - November – Men on duty at Old Harbor in November 1909 were Hezekiah F. Doane, Robert F. Pierce, Edwin P. Ellis, Otis C. Eldredge, Zebina B. Chase, Lawrence O. Hawes, Elmer L. Smith, and Richard E. Ryder. Substitute surfmen were Alpheus H. Doane and William R. Speight.

1910 - December 8 - Central heating system installed. "Heat installed at 3 pm and working fine." (From the station log.)

1911 - August 1 - Surfmen on duty as of this date were Robert F. Pierce, 155 lbs., age 45; Edwin P. Ellis, 175 lbs. age 53; Otis C. Eldredge, 165 lbs., age 55; Zebina B. Chase, 150 lbs., age 50; Elmer L. Smith, 165 lbs., age 50; and Richard E. Ryder, 170 lbs., age 32.

1911 - August 11 - At 3:30 am the lookout reported a schooner ashore on Chatham Bar, 1 1/2 miles to the south'ard. The station crew went to her in the surfboat and found her to be the 307 ton schooner *THERESA WOLF*, coal laden, bound from South Amboy, NJ for Windsor, Canada.

Photo postcard courtesy of Noel Beyle

Theresa Wolf aground at Chatham Bar

The master informed the Keeper that he had come from the shoals at 1:30 am and being in need of sleep, had given the mate the course and turned in. Two hours later he was awakened by the jar of the vessel as she grounded. He attributed the stranding to a strong current setting to the south, which swung the schooner off course. The swell bearing in over the bars caused her to pound heavily and soon set her leaking. Wreckers arrived on the scene shortly after daybreak, but she filled so rapidly it was impossible to save her. Her four-man crew, three passengers, and their personal effects were taken ashore by the lifesavers. Local men using oyster tongs later salvaged the cargo of coal.

1911 - November 6 - Surfman Robert F. Pierce, #1, was promoted to Keeper at Gay Head Life Saving Station. Jabez W. Crowell, age 35, replaced him at Old Harbor Station on November 20th.

1912 - January 9 - Went to the aid of the sharpie *ODESSA*, adrift near Strong Island.

1912 - May 1- Went to the aid of two men in a launch. In attempting to come in over the bar, the surf being very high, their boat capsized. The lifesavers went to their aid after their overturned boat was seen by the station lookout. Both men were taken to the station, where one of them received much needed medical attention. The lifesaving crew recovered the boat.

1912 - May 18 - Went to the aid of a catboat ashore south of Chatham Inlet.

1912 - June 16 - Went to the aid of the British schooner *KALEMALA* 1 ¹/₂ miles south of the station.

Drawing by Harold M. Brett, from *Life-Savers on Old Malabar*, from *Harper's Monthly*, 1907

Illustration by Chatham artist Harold M. Brett

1912 - August 30 - Went to the aid of the sloop *THYRIE*, one mile south of the station.

1912 - September 11 - Went to the aid of the catboat *PEARL B.*

1912 - September 21 - Went to the aid of a small launch, which was adrift and out of gas.

1912 - September 23 - Crew employed varnishing the boat room.

1913 - July 12 - Went to the aid of the launch *ALGONQUIN* three miles north of the station.

1913 - August 2 - The Board of Life-Saving Appliances, including the Honorable Sumner I. Kimball, General Superintendent of the Life Saving Service, were at the station to test a new type of tally board and new life belts. Kimball was familiar with the area, having been a school-teacher in Orleans early in his career.

1913 - August 10 - Went to the aid of the British schooner *PARANA*, $6^1/2$ miles south of the station. The five-man crew landed on the beach in their own boat, but the ship was lost.

1914 - January 12 - Went to the aid of the four-masted schooner *HOPE*, five miles SE of the station.

1914 - January 13 - Went to the aid of three launches caught in the ice.

1914 - August 23 - A sailing boat stranded on the beach. Surfmen took the party of five off and recovered the boat.

Old Harbor Station Crew – 1914
Capt Doane, center; Richard E. Ryder, far right. Other Surfmen known to have been on duty in August and September of 1914 were Edwin P. Ellis, age 56; Zoeth A. Sherman, age 46; Robert Robbins; Charles E. Jones; Richard F. Slavin; Isiah P. Haskins, age 41; John E. Ellis; and George B. Nickerson.

Keeper Hezekiah Doane with surfboat crew and horse

1915 - January 28 - The Revenue-Cutter Service and the Life-Saving Service were merged, and became known as the Coast Guard, by an act of Congress signed into law by President Woodrow Wilson this date.

1915 - March 22 - Keeper Hezekiah F. Doane retired after 34 years service. Keeper Doane had employed the Breeches Buoy apparatus only 4 times during his keepership at Old Harbor. Surfman #1, Richard E. Ryder, appointed as Acting Keeper.

1915 - April 7 - Joseph C. Kelley arrived and assumed his duties as Keeper. Richard E. Ryder appointed as Keeper of Monomoy Station.

CHAPTER 6

A Week at The Station
November 6-12, 1904

Things are going along smoothly at Old Harbor Station. Keeper Hezekiah Doane, age 58, has had his crew of six surfmen with him since August 1st, when the regular season began, and he has been drilling them vigorously. The "winter man", the additional surfman brought on for the winter, won't arrive for duty until the 1st of December. The weather has been typical for November on Cape Cod. There have been many cool and crisp days, with the winds coming more from the north and the amount of daylight being reduced with each passing day. On September 3rd, the station crew went to the aid of a schooner aground on Chatham Bar, but on the 13th of October last, they were unable to save the lives of the crew of the *WENTWORTH*. There is excellent team-work exhibited by the crew, but there is a sense of urgency. They don't know if any more marine disasters will occur this season, but if prior years are any indication, they do know that they will be called upon to be ever vigilant and prepared to render assistance if at all possible. All of the surfmen of Old Harbor Station were born on the lower Cape, and all have extensive boating experience in the waters of Chatham. They have been fishermen and boatmen all their lives. Most have families living on the mainland in Chatham. The men have proven themselves to Keeper Doane, and are held in high regard by him as well as the local residents. The men are used to working together in the surfboat, and are proud of what they do. Keeper Doane knows his men, and they trust him and look to him for leadership. When duty calls, he will be in the boat or at the wreck scene with them, not staying behind giving orders from a warm office. The pay for the Keeper is $900 a year; the surfmen get $65 a month. They all earn their pay.

Sunday, November 6th, 1904 - Breakfast, consisting of bacon and eggs, coffee, and apple pie, is served at 7 am. It was 40 degrees at sunrise, with a high surf running. It is cloudy, with a light northeast wind. Surfman #5 Francis H. Bassett, age 41, on liberty at 6:30 am, meets his wife Gertrude and their five daughters in North Chatham. He rowed his dory across the harbor and must return at 4 pm. When he does, he'll have the north patrol from sunset to 8 pm. H. R. Doane is assigned the day watch in the tower. He must periodically scan the horizon with binoculars or telescope, keeping an eye on all shipping in case a vessel is flying a distress signal. Doane is a substitute for Surfman Zebina B. Chase, who is temporarily disabled. It being Sunday, the rest of the men have no particular duties to perform until sunset, when the patrols resume. Several of the men are excellent duck shooters, and they spend several hours in gunning stands built on the nearby marshes. Any chance to make some extra money by market gunning is not passed up. Roast duck and geese are, of course, welcome additions to the menu at the station as well as at home. By sunset, nine brigs and eleven schooners had passed the station.

Monday, November 7th - Breakfast is served at 7 am. Bassett and Pierce have returned from the north and south patrols, while Surfman Dean Eldridge has been up in the tower since first light. It is a clear morning, 35 degrees, with a fresh breeze from the NNW. The Keeper has recorded the surf condition at sunrise as being rough, down somewhat from the high surf of yesterday. The men gather around the messroom table, talking about what went on during the night. Not much, as usual. The weather, where the good duck shooting is, and the upcoming election are the main topics of conversation. When breakfast is finished, the men carry their stoneware dishes to the kitchen, and each man takes care of washing his own. After breakfast, Keeper Doane calls for the crew to "turn to" and commence with the routine cleaning and maintenance of the station. Sunday being a day of rest, not too much was done yesterday. The floors are swept free of tracked-in sand with a corn broom, after which the plain wood floors of the messroom and kitchen are scrubbed with a stiff brush, warm water, and sal soda. It not being too late in the year to work outside, one man prepares some putty and proceeds to fix a broken window in the outbuilding. Tomorrow, if the nice weather holds, the Keeper will have the men finish painting some trim on the main building. They can paint over the fresh putty job then. Meanwhile, Surfman #1 is working with the #6 man in the boatroom. They are splicing manila rope for use on the beach apparatus cart. The Keeper is in his office taking care of paperwork and reports. At noon, lunch is ready. Once again, the crew gathers at the messroom table. Keeper Doane is known to be a very religious man, and it is his custom to say grace at the table. His usual prayer is "Heavenly Father, bestow Thy blessing. Make us truly thankful. Pardon our sins. Amen." After lunch, there are kerosene lanterns to be cleaned and filled. Before dark, coal will have to be brought inside in the coal hods, one for each stove. Ashes are taken outside and sifted through the ash sieve. The man whose turn it is to cook has finished his baking for the day, and is just about done with a nice chowder. At 4 pm, supper is served. The meal consists of fish chowder, bread, coffee, and lemon meringue pie.

"Of course, chowders were mainstays on Cape tables, but recipes for them in those old cookbooks were almost non-existent for their ingredients and composition were so taken for granted that it seemed nobody needed to be told. Ask any dyed-in-the-wool Cape Codder how to put together a fish chowder, for instance, and you may get an answer that is apt to be casual, even a trifle embarrassed, as if you had asked him his name. "Fish chowder?" he may ask. "Cod is good. Haddock is, too. Well, you take and try out some salt pork - yes, yes, try it out - fry it, y'know. Then you slice up a few onions. How many? I guess that depends on how many you're going to feed. Same with potatoes. Slice 'em up, too, kind of like thin wedges so the thin edge'll cook off and thicken the chowder. Then dump it all on top of the salt pork. With some water, you understand - not too much. Salt and a little pepper, and you let the whole thing cook up pretty slow until it's almost done. Then you lay chunks of fish on top and press 'em down good. That's got to cook a few minutes more until the fish comes apart easy and she's ready for a little milk if you want. And if you want to get real fancy, drop in a couple of pieces of butter. Nothing to it. I remember it used to taste pretty good down to the Life Saving Station after patrol on a cold January day."

From Pieces of Old Cape Cod, *by Josephine Buck Ivanoff, 1985*

Supper is served this early because the north and south patrolmen have to set out just before dark. When they come off watch at 8 pm, they and those that are hungry will eat again. It will be more coffee or tea, and perhaps some fresh gingerbread. The fellow who has "cook week" has brought his wife down to the station to help him, and all hands eat well. She sleeps in the guest bedroom on the second floor. Edwin P. Ellis, #2 man, age 47, returned from his liberty day at 4 pm, after visiting with friends in town. His return is welcome, as he had picked up the mail at the North Chatham post office before rowing back. The post office is at the corner of Old Harbor and Stony Hill Roads, about one-half mile from the Cow Yard. Walking and rowing are what these men routinely do every day. At dark, Surfman Eldridge, the day watch in the tower, comes down and joins those still sitting at the table. During the day, he sighted one bark, 50 schooners, eight steamers, and one sloop. The daylight hours have gone by quite quickly, and now it is time to play cards, checkers, or read the paper by the light of the kerosene lamp on the table. It is quiet. Other than idle conversation, there are no sounds made by man - just the rough surf rhythmically breaking on the backside and the gentle sounds of a moderate westerly breeze blowing through the beach grass. It is a peaceful place.

At 8 pm, the patrolmen with the 8-12 watch set out on their lonely walks. Pierce will head south down towards the point; substitute Surfman A. I. Doane will walk 2 $1/2$ miles up the beach to the halfway house. Surfman Mullett, the south patrolman from Orleans Station this night, will meet Doane at this marginal shelter, and they'll exchange brass tokens, or checks.

At the halfway house, they warm their hands over their patrol lanterns and exchange pleasantries. After a few minutes, they resume the patrol by heading back to their respective stations. During his watch, the beach patrolman may not stay at the station any longer than is necessary to get warm or trim his lantern. It is a clear night, with the thermometer in the high 30's, and the patrols are uneventful. Surfman D. N. Eldridge and substitute H. R. Doane have the midnight to 4 am patrols, while Surfman Ellis and substitute A. I. Doane take over from 4 am to sunrise.

Tuesday, November 8th - Election Day - At sunrise, there is a moderate northwest wind, a moderate surf, and the temperature is 35. After an early breakfast, the Keeper orders the crew to man the surfboat. This will be a drill, with the small surfboat, but the men will conduct themselves as if they were going to an actual rescue. They must be prepared to render assistance and save lives at any time. At the command "MAN THE SURFBOAT", Surfmen #5 & 6 open and secure the boatroom doors. Number 1 holds the wagon pole in position, while #2 inserts the bolt. The men fall into place with the drag ropes over their shoulders. (If a horse is used, the man who has care of it proceeds to harness it, lead it to where the boat is, and connect the harness to the boat wagon.)

Pulling the Surfboat to the Wreck Scene

Launching the Surfboat

At the command "FORWARD", the wagon is run out of the boatroom to the most desirable place for launching, as near the water as possible, the boat's bow toward the surf. At the command "HALT - UNLOAD", the drag ropes are dropped (or the horse unhitched, as the case may be, and secured at a safe place); Nos. 3 and 4 cast off the side lashings; Nos. 1, 3, and 5 on the starboard side and Nos. 2, 4, and 6 on the port side run the boat back over the rear axle as far as the wheels will allow; a surfman takes a turn with the check rope around the bilge keel or grip streak, and tends it; No. 1 swings out the starboard lifting bar; No. 2 follows with the port lifting bar, which he hooks; Nos. 1, 3, and 5 on the starboard side and Nos. 2, 4, and 6 on the port side man the bars; the Keeper removes the king bolt, the reach is lifted, the Keeper removes the forward wheels, and the reach is then carefully lowered to the ground; the check rope is slacked and the boat is slid down and off the reach; Nos. 3 and 4 then run the forward wheels and Nos. 5 and 6 the rear wheels up the beach out of the reach of the tide. Each man then takes his place on his proper side of the boat and abreast his thwart. At the command "TAKE", each man lays hold of his own life preserver. At the command "LIFE PRESERVERS", which is given shortly after the command "TAKE", the life preservers are taken simultaneously, the men put them on and proceed to adjust them. At the command "TAKE", each man lays hold of his oar. At the word "OARS", which is given after a short interval, the oars are raised simultaneously on end, blade up, and the men, governed by #1, drop them together into the rowlocks on their respective sides, the handles resting on the opposite sides of the boat. The Keeper at the same time secures the steering oar in its rowlock, its handle resting under the after thwart. (From the command "UNLOAD" until the oars were crossed and the boat was ready for launching, 30 seconds was considered ample time for a properly drilled crew to use for this evolution. On November 8th, 1904, Keeper Doane and his crew needed only 20 seconds.) At the command "GO", which the Keeper gives at his discretion, the men push the boat in to deep water as fast as they can to give the boat all headway possible, then, as it becomes waterborne, the bow oarsmen, the men amidships, and the stroke oarsman, in that order, jump in, take their oars, and give way briskly together, the bow oarsmen steadying the boat as long as the depth of the water or surf will permit, and the Keeper jumping in when he deems it best to do so.

At the command "GIVE WAY TOGETHER", all the oarsmen take the full stroke, keeping accurate stroke with the starboard stroke oar and feathering the blades. The crew pulls a strong, steady stroke, always using their backs, and maintaining silence. After the required 30 minutes of exercise at the oars, the boat is skillfully brought back through the surf to the beach. At the command "IN OARS", the oars are hauled inboard, their looms resting on the opposite rail, the men jump overboard on their respective sides and run the boat up the beach. The life preservers are removed, the oars are laid in, blades forward, and the boat is loaded on the wagon in the reverse order of unloading. (The crew was not to be drilled on loading the boat on the wagon quickly.) The boat and wagon, pulled by the men or the horse, are returned to the boatroom. Surfmen 1-4 and one substitute are given permission to be absent until noon so they can go to town to vote. The Keeper and the other substitute are absent from 2 - 4 pm, as they also wish to vote. By sunset, it is calm and clear. The watch in the tower sighted 66 schooners and eight steamers passing the station this day.

Wednesday, November 9th - At sunrise, substitute Alonzo Irving Doane takes the day watch in the tower. The surf is moderate, temperature 40 degrees, there is a light westerly wind, and it is cloudy. The Keeper departs on liberty at 7 am, leaving Pierce in charge. Keeper Doane will visit with his wife Pemah and their two sons at their home in Chatham. After breakfast, Surfman Pierce supervises the crew in signal drill. He has the men practice receiving International Morse Code by use of the occulting, or flashing, light set. They are outside the station, far enough from the light so they can't hear the clicks of the key, and they must keep track of what was sent by writing it down on paper. Pierce compares their results with what was sent and records it for the Keeper. The balance of the day is spent performing routine duties around the station. The Keeper returns from liberty at 4 pm, and places Indenting Key #1 (for the time detecting clock) in the safe at the south patrol house. By sunset, 38 schooners and eight steamers have passed the station. There is now a fresh northeast wind, the surf is moderate, the temperature is 42, and it is still cloudy. Dean Eldridge and Otis Eldredge have the sunset to 8 pm patrol; Zebina Chase (back off the disabled list) and Edwin Ellis have the 8 pm to midnight duty.

Thursday, November 10th - Surfman Pierce and substitute A. I. Doane complete their patrols at 4 am, having been relieved by Surfmen Dean Eldridge and Zeb Chase. Eldridge, age 49, departs the station at 7 am on liberty. He will visit with his wife, Lena. Surfman Edwin Ellis mans the tower. During the day, the surf condition changes from strong to rough. The wind blows moderately from the north-northeast.

After lunch, Keeper Doane calls the men to Beach Apparatus Drill. This drill was conducted weekly at all life-saving stations throughout the country. At Old Harbor, it was usually done on Thursdays. It is commonly known as the Breeches Buoy Drill, as a pair of canvas pants has been sewn on to a life ring, or buoy. The whole setup has been copied from the lifesavers on the coast of England.

The drill consists of the crew dragging the loaded practice cart to a site not far from the station.

The Keeper directs the crew as to where to place the shotline box and where the Lyle gun is to be placed. The Lyle gun is loaded with a measured charge of black powder, which when ignited, fires an 18 lb. projectile, with the shotline attached, over the "wreck pole".

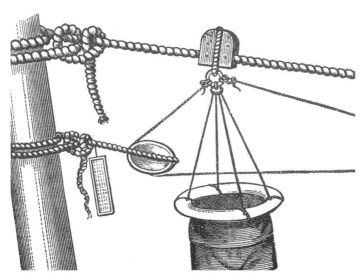

The line falls between the arms of the pole, which simulates a ship's rigging. A surfman then climbs the pole, pulls the line towards him, thus pulling the heavier whip line. This line is attached to the pole, and then that line is tied to the heavier hawser.

That is in turn pulled out to the pole and tied up as high as possible.

The breeches buoy is pulled out to the pole, clothesline fashion. The surfman steps in to it and is retrieved by his fellow surfmen who pull on the whip line. Sounds complicated, and it would be hard to expect a new surfman to know what to do just by reading the Beach Apparatus Drill manual. The weekly practice sessions were essential to maintain a competent crew.

In case of a real rescue situation, using the breeches buoy can retrieve multiple survivors quickly. It was not the preferred method of rescue, however, as the cart and equipment are difficult to drag through the snowdrifts and sand dunes. Also, there was always a doubt as to whether the shipwreck survivors would know what they had to do to be rescued.

Breeches Buoy Drill, U. S. Life Saving Station, SALISBURY BEACH, Mass.

"The Life Line" by Winslow Homer, etching from *The Century Magazine,* April 1898

From the command "ACTION" to when the #6 man was landed at the crotch during the drill today, the elapsed time recorded in the Station Log was 2 minutes, 50 seconds. Distance from crotch to pole was 55 yards. The apparatus cart used for practice this day was properly stowed and returned to the boatroom by the crew.

At sunset, Surfmen Pierce and Eldredge commence their sunset to 8 pm patrols. Ellis comes down from the tower, having seen thirteen schooners and nine steamers pass by. It is clear and 44 degrees, with rough surf and a light northeast wind. After supper, the men relax in the messroom before retiring for the night. So ends another day.

Friday, November 11 - Surfmen Pierce and Eldredge finish their 4 am to sunrise patrols, and Pierce departs on liberty at 6:40 am. He will visit his wife Minnie and their son. Sunrise found the weather to be calm and clear, temperature 42, with a moderate surf running. Zeb Chase has the tower watch, while the rest of the crew works on maintaining the station in good repair. After lunch, the keeper exercises them in the weekly drill called "Resuscitation of The Apparently Drowned". (This was a skill at which all surfmen had to be proficient, as drowning was a major cause of death in areas where the stations were located. If the victim could be reached soon enough, there was a good chance that person could be revived. The crew was required to know how to properly warm a revived victim, and how to treat frostbite. It was taught as part of this drill.) At sunset, Surfmen Bassett and Otis Eldredge commenced their sunset to 8 pm patrols. The tower watch recorded ten schooners and five steamers passing the station this day, which ended cloudy, with a light NNW wind and a moderate surf. After supper, card playing and reading the paper occupy the men.

Waiting to be rescued.

Saturday, November 12 - At sunrise, Surfmen Bassett and Pierce finish their 4 am to sunrise patrols. The surf is strong, the wind light from the west, the temperature 34. Zeb Chase, age 42, has liberty today from 6:30 to 4 pm. He plans to visit with his wife Etta and their five children. Dean Eldridge will have the watch in the tower, as well as the sunset to 8 pm patrol. Keeper Doane notes in his journal "Crew employed in routine duties." By the end of the day, 68 schooners and two steamers have passed by the station.

Thus completes a typical week in 1904 at Old Harbor Life-Saving Station. One bark, nine brigs, 256 schooners, 44 steamers, and one sloop have passed by during the daylight hours of the past seven days. None required assistance.

CHAPTER 7

The Coast Guard Era - 1915 to 1944

1915 - January 28 - The Revenue-Cutter Service and the Life-Saving Service were merged, and became known as the Coast Guard, by an act of Congress signed into law by President Woodrow Wilson this date.

The following was copied from the Old Harbor Life-Saving Station Historic Furnishings Report, Cape Cod National Seashore, 2005; *Ms. Janice Hodson, Historic Furnishings Researcher, compiled it for the U.S. Park Service.*

"The structure and make up of the Old Harbor crews slowly changed under the Coast Guard. Hezekiah Doane's retirement in 1915 after 17 years as Keeper of the station (and 34 years in the Life-Saving Service) marked the symbolic end of an era. District Superintendent George W. Bowley notified Old Harbor that Joseph C. Kelley would report for duty as the new Keeper on April 7, 1915. Old Harbor's first active season as a Coast Guard station began on August 1, 1915 and ended May 31, 1916. It was authorized to maintain a staff of one No. 1 surfman, five long-term surfmen (who would serve the entire season) and one short-term surfman (the winter man, on duty from October 1 to May 31). It was forbidden for a long-term man to be converted to a short term. By 1917 the crew at Old Harbor was increased to include the No. 1 surfman and seven additional surfmen. Traditionally the Life-Saving Service crews were made up of locals, which was certainly the case at Old Harbor. The Coast Guard logbooks include the home addresses of the enlisted men and show a marked increase in the number of non-Cape Cod residents among the crews. Through 1920, all the surfmen listed were from towns on the Cape. A year later, four out of nine crewmembers were from New Bedford, Massachusetts. As many as five temporary surfmen were hired during the summer months to offset leave and vacation time taken by the year-round staff. One Cape native who worked at Old Harbor during the early Coast Guard years was of the opinion that the crews made up of "boys signed up in Boston" were inferior to the locally hired surfmen of the Life-Saving Service years. Discipline does not seem to have been a major problem among the Old Harbor Coast Guard Station crews, although judging from the daily logs infractions for forgetting routine procedures had become more common by the 1930s. In discussing phone use at Old Harbor, the district superintendent warned "There has been altogether too much listening in and too much profane and obscene language used on this line and this office is determined to see that it is stopped immediately" and that future "offenders will be severely dealt with." Surfmen like the two who were sent to meet an associate civil engineer to transport him to Old Harbor and failed to show up at the train station were chastised for having "loitered and not paid attention to there [sic] duty" and deprived of any leave for ten days as punishment for their "performance of duty in such a slack manner". "The men that were Coast Guard, perhaps they weren't all well educated but they certainly had respect for their Keeper, that's for sure," said Rebecca Ryder when recalling her husband's service from 1906 to 1933. "There were some fellows that would drink when they were off duty and all that, but there was never any of it when they were on duty, not while Richard was Captain, I know that." During the Coast Guard years, the efficiency marks used for crew members were on a descending numerical scale: excellent, 4.0-3.5; very good, 3.5-3.0; good, 3.0-2.5; indifferent, 2.5-2.0; poor, 2.0-1.0; bad, 1.0-0. Besides skill in drills on beach apparatus, resuscitation, signals, Morse code, patrol and lookout duties, the men were marked on obedience, sobriety, health, the condition of uniforms and an individual's ability as leader of men. A monthly report on the proficiency of Old Harbor's 1922 crew shows that the seven surfmen in general received scores no lower than 2.5. The exception was Surfman No.1 who had been enlisted less than a month. Only the No.1 Surfman received an excellent to very good score in the category of leadership ability; the rest of the men ranged from indifferent to bad. In patrol and lookout duties, sobriety, obedience and health, each crewmember received a perfect score of 4. They also received consistently high marks in boat handling and beach apparatus work. Newer technologies were sometimes more difficult for the crews to master, particularly early in the Coast Guard's history. A 1917 inspection revealed that Old Harbor was among eight stations in the Second District whose crew failed to pass the occulting light signal drill. In fact, only two crewmen in the district were deemed proficient, resulting in a memo from the District Superintendent (then known as the District Commissioner) notifying Keepers to take immediate steps to rectify the situation. The Officer in Charge was penalized for an unsatisfactory mark - considered 2.0 or lower - in recitation or drill received by a crew member with at least 6 month's service. "The keeper is responsible for the proficiency of the crew in their various drills or duties and can prescribe extra drills for those who are deficient" according to a 1915 memorandum. Those crewmembers that continued to do poorly were to be reported to the District Superintendent. The Coast Guard specified those to be reported as individuals who neglected duties or were "disinclined to study or perfect themselves in their work." Infractions on the part of the Officer in Charge included "Failure to carry out drills; failure to keep screens in place or screened doors closed; to keep records in a neat and systematic manner; to maintain proper discipline, etc." An Officer was penalized for "In general, any item which lacks or indicates lack of attention on his part to his duties or lack of efficiency on the part of the crew as a whole." Things considered beyond an Officer's power to control or correct were deficient or poor equipment; poor state of repair of buildings, launchings, bulkheads (although he was expected to make recommendations as to what action should be taken); and, oddly, inefficiency in the No.1 Surfman.

As the equipment used at the station became more sophisticated, the technical skills of the crew became more specialized. On February 9, 1928 Officer in Charge A. H. Wright requested a Motor Machinist's Mate 2c (L) position be assigned to Old Harbor, which was considered third in command. Wright's justification was that the station had a motor surfboat, tractor and pumping engine that required "the entire time of one man" to be kept in good working order. "The engines are the backbone of this station and I am especially anxious to have them in high state of efficiency.... There is no doubt that the man in charge of the engine at this station has about twice as much work and responsibility as the other surfmen." Wright recommended Surfman Manter Fisher be promoted into the position, as he was "trustworthy and competent", had "a good working knowledge of gasoline engines", and was "a leading man with a strong character."

A major benefit for former Life Saving Service surfmen in the switch to the Coast Guard was the introduction of retirement benefits and pensions. Some career Life-Saving Service employees, like Doane and Ellis, remained long enough to receive pensions from the Coast Guard. Salaries, however, remained low for most men because of limited promotion opportunities within the organization. According to its 1920 annual report, the Coast Guard did not include higher grades "essential to a well-rounded military organization", which resulted in older officers with years in service "holding a rank entirely inappropriate to their age and experience" when compared with other military officers. Pay at the start of the Coast Guard years was $77 per month for the No.1 Surfman, which was raised to $83 in 1918; and $65 a month for regular surfmen (increased to $71 per month in 1918). Rebecca Ryder recalled her husband's Life Saving Service salary as being $65 a month when they were married in 1905. However, meals and uniforms were deducted from that amount. When Ryder became No. 1 Surfman at Old Harbor in 1915 he was earning $75 a month. Rebecca Ryder remembered her husband receiving his top salary in the Coast Guard when he was transferred to New York in 1918 to load ammunition from the Battery onto ships. "When he died [as Officer in Charge at Old Harbor in 1933]," she recalled, "he was getting $234 a month. During the depression, they had cut down the wages. I never knew them to do that before, and they hadn't put them back again when he died. I'm guessing that he should have been getting $250 a month."

During World War I the men were eligible to receive War-Risk insurance. In 1918, Keepers were allowed 30 days annual leave and surfmen

15 days. Ten days re-enlistment leave was granted to surfmen re-enlisting after January 15 plus the 15 days annual leave. Rebecca Ryder recalled the Keepers being able to carry over unused leave days. In contrast to the one day a week of leave given to a single crew member on a rotating basis during the Life Saving Service years, by 1942 generally three men at a time were away from the station on 48 hour liberty. This was made possible because of the larger size of the crew and the almost exclusive use of Coast Guard cutters for major rescues by this time.

Despite these advantages, a higher rate of crew turnover began by the 1920s, perhaps due to enlisted men frequently relocating or obtaining positions in other branches of the government. In dramatic contrast to its Life-Saving Service days when one man served as Keeper for 17 years, Old Harbor had eight Officers in Charge between 1923 and 1944. Most of these transient men only served one to two years before being reassigned. In 1920 the Coast Guard cited the lack of advancement as causing problems in retaining young officers. As enlisted men, crewmembers had a wider range of employment options within the Coast Guard and outside the government. When Surfman Herbert Gould's term of enlistment expired on March 31, 1928 he chose not to reenlist. Wright wrote "I have complied with the Regulations in every respect, explaining the advantages of the service in general. Gould was my first choice for Motor M.M.2c (L), but [on] account of above was not recommended. This was known to him but he still remains determined to leave." When Surfman Lester Taylor was discharged in 1928, he received a suit of civilian clothing - coat, pants and cap - purchased by the station from Puritan Clothing Co. in Chatham.

Medical attention for surfmen improved under the Coast Guard. Enlisted men were treated at the Marine Hospital in Boston. Periodic visits to the stations by medical professionals are noted in the logbooks. A May 29, 1916 memo informed Keeper Kelley that Senior Surgeon Fairfax Irwin of the U.S. Public Health Service was to visit all Second District stations to provide medical treatment to warrant officers and enlisted men. Still, work-related illnesses remained prevalent. Jabez Crowell, who had been No.1 Surfman at Old Harbor in 1913, retired on March 3, 1916 after having been ill since the previous August. He was about 40 years old. L. C. Mullet, who had become ill in September 1915, retired on March 31, 1916. Like Crowell, he never returned to the station after becoming sick. The log entry for March 4, 1923 recorded that the American flag at the station was lowered to half-mast during the funeral of No. 2 Surfman W. E. Harding. Harding, an Old Harbor crewmember since 1921 whose health had been ranked excellent in 1922, had become ill on February 22. On February 28, Boatswain J. DeGroot wrote, "At 2:30 received word from contract Physician J. B. Worthing that Surfman W. C. Harding had passed away. Cause of death: pneumonia. Reported matter to the District Superintendent." Harding's appears to have been the first death of a surfman on active duty in Old Harbor's history (it might have been a result of the Spanish flu epidemic). By the end of the Coast Guard era, regular check-ups and inoculations had become standard.

Despite advancements in transportation, health care and pensions, the physical risk of the job and the prolonged separation from close relatives remained as painful during the Coast Guard years as it had during the Life-Saving Service era. The families of many crewmembers spoke of the difficulties of having husbands and sons employed as lifesavers. "It was an unhappy day for her when I signed up," Alvin Wright said of his wife. Lydia Wright spoke of worrying about her husband, having bad dreams and enduring the isolation: "It was very lonely. I was a city girl and it was hard to live on the Cape all alone, especially before the children were born."

Wright enlisted in the Coast Guard as a temporary surfman at Old Harbor in 1916. He had at one time been in the Life-Saving Service but had resigned. His stint at Old Harbor was intended to be temporary: "I told my wife, I'll go down and stay a month, then when the fishing is better, I'll come home." Wright remained at Old Harbor Station for at least 15 years. "I loved that station," he said of Old Harbor. "It was my favorite of them all." He was Officer in Charge from 1926 -1931. "I liked the life. I liked the beach," he told an interviewer. "Oh, each year I'd threaten to get out, but I never did. My yearly tour was up in June, and in June the beach is beautiful. The beach peas are out. They are purple and the vines cover the sand. So I'd say, 'Oh, well, I'll try it for another year.'" At the time of his retirement in 1949, Wright had served in the Coast Guard over 32 years."

Old Harbor Coast Guard Station activities from 1915 continue:

1915 - March 22 - Keeper Hezekiah F. Doane retired after 34 years service. Surfman #1 Richard E. Ryder appointed as Acting Keeper.

1915 - April 7 - Joseph C. Kelley arrived and assumed his duties as Keeper. Richard E. Ryder appointed as Keeper of Monomoy Station.

1915 - August 3 - A skiff adrift was picked up.

1915 - August 20 - The crew was employed mowing salt hay to be used for bedding for the horse.

1915 - August 25 - Gave aid to dory fisherman John Pierce of Boston, who had lost his vessel and had rowed two days to reach land.

1915 - September 21 - Picked up the skiff *DESIRE* in the breakers with one person on board and towed it into the harbor.

1915 - September 27 - Found a skiff adrift; recovered it and turned it over to the owner.

1916 - January 19 - The schooner *LAVINIA M. SNOW* lost her chains and anchor in a gale. After rowing off to the vessel at 7 am, the station crew sent out a call for the nearest cutter and a message to her owners.

1916 - January 22 - Practiced with the fire apparatus. Time: 1 ¹/₄ minutes; water thrown 50 feet with 2 ¹/₂" hose.

1916 - July 6 - Received a 26-foot gasoline powered surfboat. Keeper Kelley went in his own powerboat to Meetinghouse Pond in Orleans to tow the new boat back. Fred W. Fulcher had transported the new surfboat from the Orleans depot to the pond.

1916 - September 7 - Station horse shot by orders of the District Superintendent. The horse had been lame since July and was being carefully treated by the crew, but he did not improve. Dr. Pope, the veterinarian, was summoned and recommended that the horse be destroyed. This was accomplished at 10 am, with burial at 2 pm.

1916 - October 5 - Keeper Kelley walked halfway to Orleans to pick up a new horse. Later in the day he made the terse log entry "Horse is sick."

1916 - November 21 - An unnamed motorboat parted her moorings and became stranded. The station crew hauled her up on the beach.

1917 - April 4 - A new line was put on a skiff that had parted her line and become stranded a third of a mile NW of the station.

1917 - June 15 - A steamer towing two barges was warned away from shore by the patrol burning a Coston signal.

1917 – August 19 - An unnamed motor boat with nine persons on board went on Pollock Rip Shoal, ten miles south of the station, and sank. The crew escaped in a boat. The occupants were picked up by the station crew and succored for the night.

1917 - August 20 - Two steamers, one mile NE of the station, were warned away from shore by the patrol burning a Coston signal.

1917 - September 29 - Crew employed in painting the hallway from the tower to the lower floor. Used 1 ¹/₂ gallons of #34 Navy green paint.

1917 - November 6 - A rowboat was found adrift two miles NW of the station, evidently abandoned. There was no trace of the boatman and the boat was recovered.

1918 - April 3 - Two steamers, one mile ESE of the station, were warned away from shore by Coston signal.

1918 - May 4 - A steamer one mile east of the station was warned away from shore by Coston signal.

1918 - July 25 - Men on duty at this time included George B. Nickerson, Carlton E. Long, Alvin H. Wright, Leroy C. Hopkins, Victor C. Cahoon, Leon F. Stevens, Richard B. Hamilton, and Richard J. Glendon

1918 - August 6 - A sick man was carried to Chatham from the 98-ton schooner *HESPER*.

1918 - August 17 - Received a speaking tube system, enabling communication from the tower to the messroom.

1918 - September 11 - A steamer one half mile NE of the station was warned away from shore by use of a Coston signal.

1919 - January 23 - A steamer two miles NNE of the station was warned away from shore by Coston signal.

1919 - January 31 - A steamer one mile SE of the station was warned away from shore by Coston signal.

1919 - February 2 - A skiff was found adrift several miles NW of the station. It was picked up and restored to the owner.

1919 - April 13 - A steamer a half mile north of the station was warned away from shore by Coston signal.

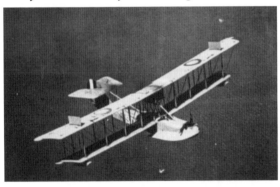

Navy Curtiss HS2L Seaplane - U.S. Navy Photo

1919 - August 28 - Navy HS2L seaplane #2241 became stranded four miles north of the station. It was pulled clear by the Old Harbor station crew during a pre-dawn high tide and towed to the Naval Air Station at Chathamport.

The famed NC-4 - an early Navy Seaplane also built by Curtiss. This plane landed off Chatham in 1918 and taxied up Pleasant Bay to the Naval Air Station for repairs while enroute to the Azores during the first transatlantic flight. LT Elmer Stone, U.S. Coast Guard, piloted the plane.

1919 - November 7 - The Old Harbor Station Motor Surfboat, #1379, broke her moorings in rough seas and went ashore one mile south of Chatham Station, on Monomoy. The boat was taken to safety and later returned to her mooring with assistance from the Chatham Station crew.

1919 - December 11 - A motorboat with one person on board was left dry on the meadow 1 1/2 miles NE of the station. It was launched by the station crew using planks and rollers.

1920 - May 8 - Received dory #1729 from H. Lowell & Son, Amesbury, Mass.

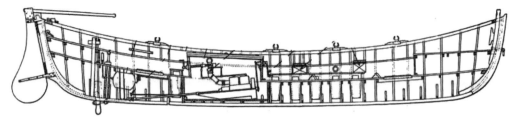

26' Lapstrake Motor Surfboat, similar to Motor Surfboat #1379. The boat was powered by a 2 cycle, three cylinder "Aristox" make and break engine.

Boat plan and photo from the National Archives, courtesy of Tim Dring, Lifeboat Historian

1920 - July 7 - A small sailboat with two persons on board became stranded ³/₄ mile north by east of the station. She was pulled clear and taken to a pier in Chatham.

1920 - August 12 - A raft broke away from her moorings, was picked up a half mile SE of the station and towed ashore.

1920 - November 16th to 20th - World War I Victory Medals were awarded to Boatswain Mate 1st Class G. B. Nickerson, Surfman #2 A. H. Wright, and Warrant Boatswain Joseph C. Kelley.

1920 - November 17 - A motorboat went ashore one mile west of the station in a strong breeze. The station crew refloated her.

1920 - November 26 - The motorboat *LYDIA* fouled her anchor and dragged ashore ³/₄ mile west of the station. After clearing her anchor, the station crew refloated her at high tide and anchored her in deep water.

Old Harbor Crew with Surfboat in Pleasant Bay, about 1920
L to R: Bill Nelson; Darby Harding; Officer in Charge Alvin Wright; Unknown surfman; Warren Baker
Photo from Cape Cod National Seashore archives

1921 - June 27 - The sloop *SEAL* was found at anchor, with no one on board, a half mile east of Chatham Station. She was towed into Chatham harbor and anchored. Later, at the request of the owner, she was towed out of the harbor.

1921 - June 29 - The motorboat *LACONIA*, with two persons on board, was towed into the harbor and anchored in a safe place after her motor became disabled.

NOTE: From July 1st, 1921, the Annual Reports become much more sparse and do not list all the assistance provided by various Coast Guard ships and stations. The remainder of this Chapter is not a complete listing of assistance rendered, but does give a decent idea of life at the station in the 20s and 30s. With more commercial vessels becoming powered with engines instead of sail and the construction of the Cape Cod Canal, the number of serious strandings and wrecks became fewer. The amount of assistance provided to pleasure boaters increased markedly. As will be seen, there were exceptions to the daily routine of drills, painting, and cleaning.

1921 - August 14 - An underwater telephone cable was laid across Chatham Harbor, connecting Old Harbor Station with Chatham Station. This was a replacement for an earlier cable laid in July 1901.

The new cable was comprised of a single copper wire encased in insulation, then surrounded by a fibrous wrapping, then finally protected by the heavy steel wires as shown. This piece of the telephone cable was found buried in the sand south of the former Old Harbor Station site.

1922 – October 12 - Received a Fordson Track-son tractor. Now the crew could retire the horse and use the tractor to pull the surfboat to the scene of a wreck.

Photo from the National Archives, courtesy of Tim Dring, Lifeboat Historian

In a letter dated December 1st, 1922, Coast Guard headquarters decreed, "Bottoms of boats regularly kept out of the water should be painted green below the water line."

1922 – October 30th - Surfmen on duty at this time are: A. H. Wright, W. W. Baker, W. C. Harding, D. E. Howes, W. M. Nelson, J. M. Hinchey, and J. A. Souza.

1924 – February 7th – "At 5:00 a.m. temporary surfman J. M. Hinchey reported a steamer ashore. Officer in charge ordered a Coston signal burned, which was done. Two rockets were fired from steamer and were answered by Coston signals. Went to shore and decided it was too rough to launch a boat before daylight. Notified the cutter *ACUSHNET* at Woods Hole at 5:45 a.m. The officer on watch said it would be about one hour before they could get under weigh. Notified District Superintendent by telephone. Communicated with steamer by occulting light, learning that steamer was the *PANUCO* of the Ward Line, from Matanzas, Cuba for Boston, Mass. (with $552,000 worth of sugar) and that steamer was not leaking and in good condition."

At 6:00 a.m. launched surfboat No. 375 and went on board steamer. Learned from the captain that Chatham Lighthouse was mistaken for Highland Lighthouse. The officers all claimed that they were not informed of the change of the character of Chatham Lighthouse."

(Note: According to the Barnstable Patriot, *Chatham Twin Light's characteristics had, in fact, been changed about nine months earlier. On or about May 15th, 1923, in the south tower there was to be one flashing white light, showing a group of four flashes every 30 seconds. This was in anticipation of the removal of the north tower to the Nauset Beach Light Station.)*

The Captain asked what their chances were for getting off. Officer in charge informed him that steamer would undoubtedly go afloat before high tide. There being no assistance that station crew could render, came ashore at 8:00 a.m. At 11:05 steamer was afloat and clear of bar. Cutter was notified by radio that steamer was afloat and that her assistance was not required. The cutter had approached within about three miles of steamer when steamer went afloat."

Signed: G. B. Nickerson, Officer in Charge

1924 – February 23rd – "Upon return from leave was informed that there was a five masted barkentine at anchor seven miles ENE from this station with a signal flying which was thought to be a two flag signal." *(Flag signals using only two flags were Distress Signals.)* "Sent Surfmen White and Laporte to town for Surfman Ellis, who was on liberty. During this time tractor was being filled with water and engine being warmed up, and sail to surfboat reefed. The three surfmen returned at noon."

"At 12:30 P.M. launched surfboat No. 375. At 3:15 P.M., after a hard pull went on board barkentine" 284-foot *MALFETTA* bound from Norfolk, VA. to Boston with $34,000 worth of coal. "Was informed by the master that he got under weigh at 6:00 P.M. Feb 22nd from anchorage near this station. Got up off Cape Cod Light when a squall blew away his fore and mizzen sails, which obliged to return where anchored. Was also (informed) that windlass was damaged in the gale Feb 20th but had been temporarily repaired, and also that the vessel was short of provisions. Returned to station at 5:45 P.M."

"Notified District Superintendent by telephone, who was to inquire if tug had been or was to be sent to assist barkentine. At 8:00 P.M. District Superintendent telephoned that *ACUSHNET* was going to the assistance of barkentine. The *ACUSHNET* arrived alongside barkentine at 11:00 A.M. Feb. 24th. At 11:45 A.M., barkentine was in tow, bound to the northward".

Signed: G. B. Nickerson, Officer in Charge

Authors comment: Note that the surfboat was rigged for sail, and that the "hard pull" mentioned by the Officer In Charge took two hours and 45 minutes. Also, the proper spelling of the vessel was MOLFETTA.

The completed barkentine *MOLFETTA* at Pascagoula, Mississippi, about 1920.

Photo from *The Italian-American Shipyard at Pascagoula*, Richard W. Bricker

1926 - June 5th through 9th – Services rendered to Boston fishing vessel *MARITIMA* - "At 9:30 P.M. Surfman W. J. LaPorte, having station lookout watch reported a vessel dangerously close in, abreast station. Coston signal burned at once. Vessel did not change course; burned two more Coston signals; vessel did not change course and stranded (?) mile NE of station. Manned surfboat No. 375 at once, boarded vessel and took crew of seven ashore to station. Called cutter *ACUSHNET* at 11:40 P.M. and again at 7:00 A.M. the 6th instant. Being informed that *ACUSHNET* could not come. Reason for stranding: did not make proper allowance for drift during a time motor was disabled while coming from South Shoal Lightship, where vessel had been fishing. Vessel lies dry at low water.

Received following message from cutter *TUSCARORA*:

"Please telephone Old Harbor Station, ascertaining present condition of small sailing vessel ashore near there."

Cutter *TUSCARORA* – Coast Guard photo

"At 6:50 P.M. 7th instant cutter *TUSCARORA* arrived off station; set International Code Signal FH, "Send Boat". Answered same and went on board at (?):50 A.M. Commanding Officer of cutter decided not to make an attempt to float stranded vessel this date. Returned to station at 3:50 P.M.

"At (?):10 the 8th instant cutter signaled "send men to vessel to take our line." Launched surfboat No. 375, took No. 9 shotline from cutter's boat ashore, hauled in 3 inch line, 4 inch line, 6 inch line, 8 inch line, then got 10 inch hawser within 125 feet of stranded vessel. As far as it could be hauled by tractor at this time. All lines were hauled in by tractor except shotline."

"At 3:45 P.M. went on board cutter at request of commanding officer. Made arrangements for signaling when cutter was ready to pull on vessel at high water. At 4:00 P.M. came ashore and got straps around vessel. Got 10-inch hawser to vessel's stern, made secure and signaled cutter "All Fast". Returned to station at 7:30 P.M."

"At 9:30 P.M. went to stranded vessel to keep watch of progress made in attempt to float her and signal same to cutter. At 10:20 P.M. cutter signaled "Ready to Pull". Signaled cutter to "Pull Away". At 11:00 P.M. vessel pulled afloat. Signaled cutter "Vessel Afloat". Cutter started northward at 1:25 A.M. June 9th with *MARITIMA* in tow."

G. B. Nickerson, Officer In Charge

Report noted "Rough sea made it difficult to run lines and for cutter to get in near enough for hawser to reach vessel." Also, that they lost two tension bolts for the caterpillar tread on the tractor.

1926 – July 26th – Fordson tractor and truck cart employed to retrieve stranded skiff.

1926 – August 24th – Provided towing assistance at the Chatham Bar to the Provincetown dragger *FOUR BROTHERS*, Charles Joseph, Master.

1926 – September 11th – Provided towing assistance with the power surfboat to the Harwichport power dory #171-D in trouble at the Chatham Bar.

1926 – September 25th – Conducted unsuccessful search for a small catboat declared missing by owner.

1926 – December 3rd – Steamer warned by Coston flares that it was anchored too close to the outer bar.

1926 – December 8th – Schooner collision:

"At 11:25 a.m. Surfman H. W. Gould, on lookout duty, reported two schooners, a three and four master, seven miles east of station in apparent distress. The fourmast schooner had signal hoisted which could not be made out; threemast schooner had flag in main rigging Union down."

"Launched power surfboat No. 2890 at 1250 pm, left harbor at 1:00 p.m. Arrived to three masted schooner at 2:00 pm. Name – *AMY G. McKEAN*, from Country Harbor, Nova Scotia; lumber laden, bound for Bridgeport, Conn.; Master H. E. Hilton, who stated that the fourmasted schooner laying at this time 1 mile NE from his vessel collided with him off Rose and Crown Shoal at 9 pm. December 7th, carrying away his mizzenmast, shifting his house over a foot and staving the vessel in, just above the waterline on Port quarter. Vessel leaking but not seriously. Requested Cutter be sent to tow him in. No further assistance required. Left the *AMY G. McKEAN* for four masted schooner at 2:15 p.m."

"Left the three masted schooner *AMY G. McKEAN* for fourmasted schooner laying 1 mile NE; arrived to four masted schooner *VELMA L. HAMLIN* at 2:45 pm. Vessel lumber laden, from Cape Breton to New York. Master Captain Sweeney of Boston, who stated that he collided with three masted schooner, laying 1 mile SW of him at present time, at 9 pm December 7th off Rose and Crown Shoal, carrying away his jibboom bowsprit, foremast head and all jibs. Vessel unmanageable; requested that a cutter be sent to tow him to Vineyard Haven. Returned to station at 3:50 pm."

Signed: A. H. Wright, Officer in Charge

Type H Motor Surfboat, similar to Old Harbor boat #2890.
Based on available records, the boat is presumed to have been built in 1926 at the Coast Guard Yard in Curtis Bay, MD.
Photo from the National Archives, courtesy of Tim Dring, Lifeboat historian

1927 – July – Boats on hand at this time were: Self Bailing Motor Surfboat #2890 built in 1926; Monomoy pulling boat #375, built in 1898; Monomoy pulling boat #457, built in 1900; 15 foot fisherman's dory #729; and 13 foot fisherman's dory #2194. In August, in the opinion of the Officer in Charge, surfboat #457 was unfit for further service.

1928 – March 24th – Coal requirements for Fiscal Year 1929 were projected to be 10 tons of nut coal for the kitchen range and 15 tons of Franklin egg coal for the furnace. Suggested suppliers were Charlie Harding & Horace Bearse of Chatham, or Harry Snow of Orleans.

1928 – April 26 – Clothing provided by the Women's National Relief Association was supplied to five members of the sunken schooner *WILLIAM BOOTH* by the station crew. The 170-foot long, three-masted *WILLIAM BOOTH*, stone laden, was cut down and sunk by the four-master *HELEN BARNET GRING*.

Alleged rumrunner *MARIA DEL SOCCORSA* aground on a sandbar, early 1930s. Crews from the Orleans and Old Harbor stations boarded her.

Cape Cod National Seashore archive photo

Men on duty in the tower during the Coast Guard era kept rough logbooks for later examination by the Officer in Charge. Some pages were written in pencil and are difficult to read, while others in ink are still quite legible. The page shown was written on November 3rd, 1930. Coast Guardsmen making entries on this page are: R. C. Hopkins, Surfman #2; G. H. Marshall, #3; Joseph A. Flores, #9; H. W. Watkins, #7; George Williams, #6; E. D. Long, #8.

Other members of the crew on the station at this time were: A. H. Wright, Officer in Charge; S. W. Fisher, Boatswains Mate 1st Class (Lifesaving), Surfman #1; C. E. Shupe, #4; John E. Munson, #10; Lawrence Enos, #9; and John Andrews, Machinists Mate 2nd Class, #2. Mention is often made of a surfman reporting to the tower by phone from the "North Patrol House", and through the period of the book the numbers assigned to the men often change.

Day to day entries in the book that cover the period Sept 30th, 1930 through February 17th, 1931 usually record Chatham fishermen coming and going, the weather conditions, and vessel traffic along the coast. There is a list of Coast Guard cutters and their numerals on the inside front of the book. Apparently this was to enable watch standers to readily identify the cutters as they cruised by the station. Cutters named include: CG-2 *CONYNGHAM*, CG-13 *JOUETT*, CG-17 *PAULDING*, CG-24 *WAINWRIGHT*, and CG-20 *TRIPPE*. These "4 stacker" cutters were capable of a top speed of 29 knots, and were on loan to the Coast Guard from the U.S. Navy for use in enforcing laws dealing with Prohibition.

Photo courtesy of Williamn P. Quinn

Coast Guard Cutter *PAULDING*

1931 - August 31 - Surfman Marshall records "U.S. dirigible *LOS ANGELES* bound south." This sighting must have made his day.

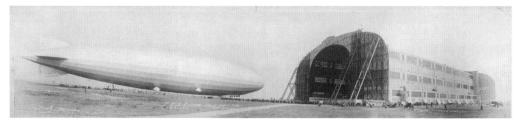

Dirigible *LOS ANGELES*, ZR3, entering hangar at Lakehurst, NJ, 1924
Library of Congress/R. S. Clements, Photographer

Merry Xmas

Dec. 25, 1931

tower equipment o.k.
No shipping.
R. M. Mason

Dec 25. 1931
2:30 Telescope, Binoculars, & watch clock
in good condition
Geo. Marshall

Dec 25. 1931
4:30 Telescope Binoculars & watchclock
in good condition
6:00 Line reported On K. South
West-1-29- — -7-M
Geo. Williams.

Dec. 25. 1931
Log West - 1-30 44 — 219 — F — M.
Telescope + Binoculars + Watch Clock in
good Condition No Shipping
Thick Fogg.
Walter M. Knowles Surfman no 9

Dec 25, 1931
tower equipment o.k.
2:45 Steamer bound north.
3:25 Steamer bound north.
Log WNW-3-29:41-46-R-M
R. Mason

Dec. 25, 1931
6:00 Telescope, Binoculars + watchclock
in good condition
5:4 Steamer bound South
Geo. Williams

12/25/31
7:00 Marshall Reported N. Patrol
8:00 Tower Equipment ok.
8:00 Log NW S-29-50-41-0-M
Jwo watkins
G H Marshall

Entries in the logbook covering the period August 4th, 1931 to March 6th,
1932 now include that the telescope, binoculars and watch clock are in good
condition. Men making entries now include Phil Packet, #8;
Walter M. Knowles, #9; and J. A. Serpa.

1932 – October 29th – A gunning dory "was noticed drifting dangerously near Chatham Bars while coot shooting. Thinking perhaps they were inexperienced oarsmen and a very strong current was setting out of harbor, I thought I would run down (in the Motor Surfboat #2890) and find out if they were in any danger. They were at anchor when I arrived at scene, but each time anchor was lifted to pick up a bird, they were drifting nearer to the breakers. I asked them if they could pull back against the strong wind and current, and one answered yes, when the tide turned. When I informed him that the tide would not turn till after dark, they were very grateful to be towed back under beach, where the shooting was good and much smoother water. Returned to station about 2:40 p.m., after loaning them a thole pin as they were one short."

Signed: R. E. Ryder, Boatswain (L), Officer in Charge.
Boat crewmen were Surfmen E. D. Long and L. F. Enos

1932 – November 10 – Allis-Chalmers Model MU Crawler Tractor, Coast Guard Motor Vehicle #1049, arrived.

This tractor replaced the Fordson-Trackson, and was used to pull the surfboat wagon to the wreck scene. Also, the crew could use it to tow a wagon while picking up firewood washed up on the beach. The machine was powered with a 4-cylinder gas engine, had a 6-volt starter and electrical system, and a top forward speed of 4.25 mph. It was painted with a special Coast Guard-prescribed paint formulation of aluminum bronze powder mixed with varnish. Optional items that were on other Outer Cape Coast Guard tractors included engine covers and a power-take-off drum in the front.

During the period March 1933 until December, 1933, men at Old Harbor included: Fred Wheldon, #7; F. Silva, #3; H. Watkins, #4; G. H. Marshall, #2; R. Mason, #6; L. DeCosta, #8; N. L. Ross, #8; L. F. Enos, #8; S. M. Fisher, #1; E. D. Long, #5; W. B. Murphy, #9; and R. E. Small.

Surfman Frederick H. Wheldon

Warrant Boatswain (L) Richard E. Ryder was Officer in Charge from June 1932 until his death on June 8th, 1933. Chief Boatswain John E. Wescott took his place until Arthur E. Larkin took over in April 1934.

"He was a man whose integrity has never been questioned, and was greatly respected by all who had the privilege of knowing him; a man whose personality inspired trust, confidence and justice. The untimely death of Boatswain (L) R. E. Ryder was a great shock to the entire community, and to service men in general."

Sherwood M. Fisher, Acting Officer in Charge, 18 June, 1933

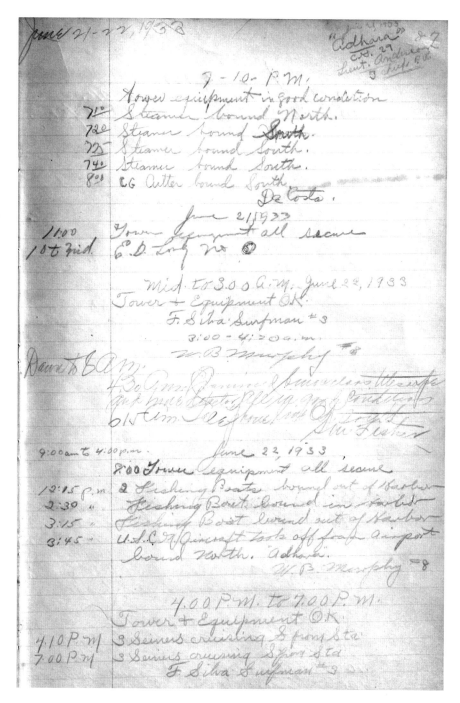

1933 - June 22nd – Page of Tower Logbook. Note that the 3:45 entry reads, "U.S.C.G. aircraft took off from airport bound North. '*ADHARA.*'" This plane was a nearly new twin engine Douglas RD2 amphibian.

It was seen the day after as well, "Circling over bay". The plane's name, as well as her pilot's name, (LT Anderson) is also noted on the upper right corner of this logbook page. One wonders if the plane taxied up to the station and the aircrew paid a visit!

The RD-2 *ADHARA* was commissioned in 1932 and was based in Gloucester in 1933 and subsequent years until she crashed in 1937. Seeing a new Coast Guard amphibian must have been exciting for the crew of Old Harbor Station.

Coast Guard amphibian *ADHARA*
June 14th, 1932

Photo from US Coast Guard Aviation History file

Photo from US Coast Guard Aviation History file

Radio gear aboard *ADHARA*. Main transmitter 100 watts, 285-600 Kc.; CW and voice transmitter 5 watts, 2464-4050 Kc.; CGR-19-C radio direction finder.

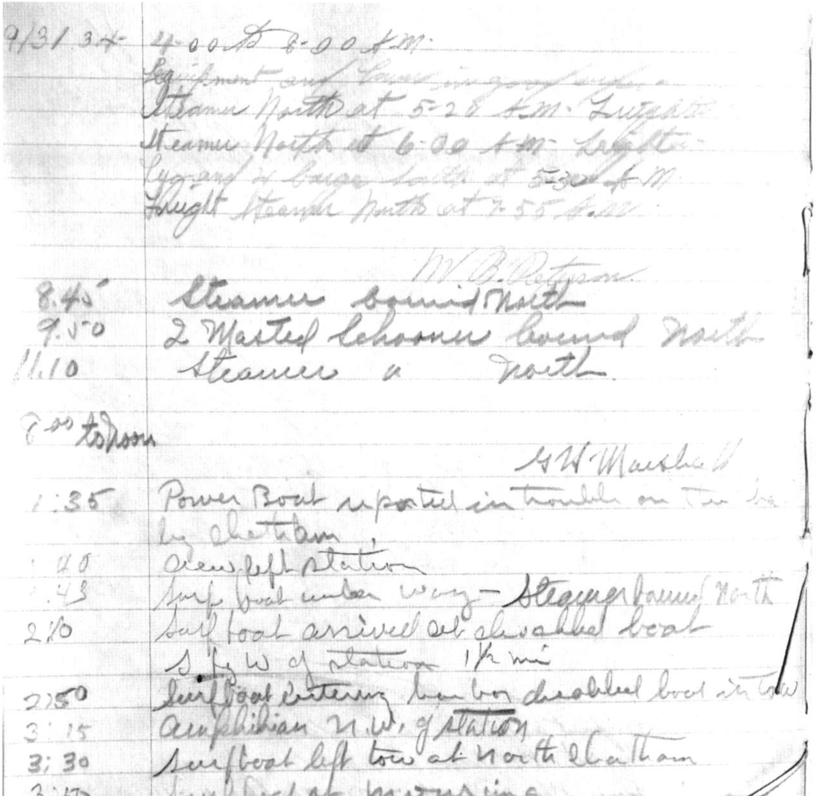

9/31/34 4.00 to 8.00 A.M.
Equipment and Gear in good order.
Steamer North at 5.28 A.M.
Steamer North at 6.00 A.M.
Barge south at 5.30 A.M.
Freight Steamer North at 7.55 A.M.
M.B. Peterson

8.45 Steamer bound North
9.50 2 Masted Schooner bound North
11.10 Steamer " North

8.00 to Noon
G.H. Marshall

1:35 Power Boat reported in trouble on the bar by Chatham.
1.40 Crew left station
1.43 Surf boat under way — Steamer bound North
2.10 Surf boat arrived at disabled boat S by W of station 1½ mi
2.50 Surf boat entering harbor disabled boat in tow
3:15 Amphibian N.W. of station
3:30 Surfboat left tow at North Chatham
3:50 Surfboat at mooring
130 – 4.00 H.W. Watkins

9/3/34 4.00 to 8.00 P.M.
Equipment and Gear in good order.
Log in poor condition
Sloop out harbor at 4.30 P.M.
Sloop up harbor at 4.35 P.M.
Sea-plane South at 4.35 P.M.
Sea Plane South at 4.50 P.M.
Sloop up harbor at 5.00 P.M.
Schooner down harbor at 5.10 P.M.
Powerboat up harbor at 5.10 P.M.
Steamer North at 5.10 P.M.
Steamer South at 6.10 P.M.
Biplane North at 6.15 P.M.
Steamer South at 7.35 P.M. (Passenger)
M.B. Peterson

1934 – September 31 - Entries in the Rough Logbook above show the crew towing in a disabled boat.

Men making entries in the Old Harbor Rough Logbook during the period December 1933 through September 1934 include:
S.M. Fisher; Spaulding; G.H. Marshall; H.W. Watkins; F. Silva; L.F. Enos; E.D. Long; R.E. Small; L. DeCosta and M.B. Peterson.

1937 – July - Personnel changes at Old Harbor during the month included Officer in Charge Yngve Rongner reenlisting for three years and Ralph Q. Bliven arriving from Monomoy Station. Lawrence DeCosta, Prince E. Goodspeed and Edward A. Tucker took annual leave.

1939 – Early February - From the *Barnstable Patriot* newspaper:
"The second shipwreck of the winter on Nauset Beach occurred early Friday morning (February 3rd) when the British motor ship *LUTZEN* struck. Attempting to row ashore in a dory one seaman was drowned. The tragedy occurred within one hundred yards of the spot where the Boston trawler *ANDOVER* grounded in late December. Her hulk lies rotting there in the sands and it looks as if the *LUTZEN* too had found her last resting place. Thick weather caused the *LUTZEN* to stray off course. She was en route from Halifax, Nova Scotia, to New York with a cargo of frozen blueberries, salmon and cod liver oil."

Cape Cod Standard-Times photo, courtesy of William P. Quinn

Steamer *LUTZEN* aground near Old Harbor station.

The steel hulled, 155-foot long freighter *LUTZEN* came ashore during thick fog. The crew of Old Harbor Station, under the command of Chief Boatswain Charles R. Ellis, removed the remaining members of the crew by surfboat. Local men were hired to remove the cargo. In doing so, the starboard side was offloaded first as she lay parallel to the beach, facing south. The ill-fated vessel rolled over on her port side and salvage of the complete ship was impossible.

Cape Cod Standard-Times photo, courtesy of William P. Quinn

According to a 1937 article in the *New York Times*, the *LUTZEN* had a history of bad luck. On January 10th, 1937, her skipper, Capt. George Rideout, was swept overboard and lost during a gale while trying to lash down a lifeboat. The ship was headed to New York from Halifax, Nova Scotia.

From the *Christian Science Monitor*:

"PHILADELPHIA, Nov. 17th 1937 - The tiny Newfoundland trawler. *LUTZEN*, famous in Southampton, England for her annual voyages across the Atlantic with a hold filled with salmon, docked at Philadelphia after battling mountainous seas on her regular autumn trip from St. John's with a cargo of Newfoundland blueberries. Tied up at Pier D, with salt crusting her funnel like frozen spray, the vessel looked more like a river tug than a ship at home anywhere in the North Atlantic. "We ran into the stormiest weather I ever saw this time," said the skipper, Newton Halfyard. "Our decks were awash most of the time. Waves pounded as high as our wheelhouse. We had a little engine trouble while the seas were tossing us about like a cork and we put into Halifax for repairs on the way down." The *LUTZEN*'s net tonnage is only 229. Her 350-horsepower engine gives her an average speed of nine knots."

1939 – August – Men on duty around this time included Yngve Rongner, Edgar Dorian, Harold Simmons, Edric Young, Francis Russo, Lawrence DeCosta, and Edward Preston, Jr. Motor Surfboats #1399 and 4022 are mentioned, and on November 7th, the crew practiced under oars in the "Race Point" surfboat.

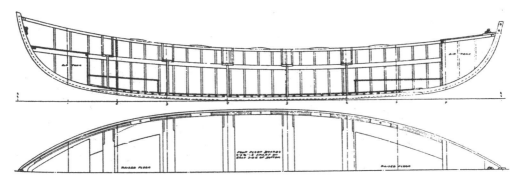

Race Point Model Surfboat

1939 – October 3rd – During the night, a Force 8 Northeast gale caused Dory #4672 to go adrift from its mooring. George Goodspeed down at Inward Point on Monomoy found it, in pieces. On the 17th, LCDR F. B. Lincoln arrived to conduct an investigation regarding the loss of the dory.

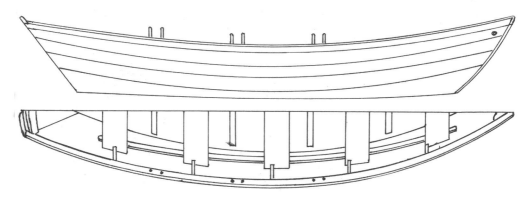

Coast Guard Dory

1940 – September 13th – Motor Surfboat #4022 was towed by Motor Surfboat #5150 to the bell buoy off Chatham Bar and delivered to the cutter *GENERAL GREENE* for delivery to the Coast Guard depot.

Photo taken by Albert F. Collins – Cape Cod National Seashore Collection

Old Harbor Coast Guard Station - about 1940

The truck was used almost daily to take men off the beach for their 48 hour liberty, to get groceries and mail, and to retrieve men returning from leave. On a trip to Orleans on January 28th, 1941, the truck was nearly submerged in soft wet sand, after which it was towed out with the tractor. It had to be totally taken apart, dried out, and cleaned up. The crew had it back together and running again on the 31st.

At left: Joseph White,
Chief Boatswains Mate, USCG
Officer in Charge from May 1940
until December 31st, 1940

Photo courtesy of
Warrant Boatswain Milton Steele,
USCG, Retired

The following men served as Officer in Charge after Boatswain White:

- Magnus Peterson, Dec. 31, 1940 until December, 1941
- Louis Silva, December 1941 until ?
- Harvey Bloomer, 1942 ? until April 1943
- John Taves, April 1943 until January 1944
- From January 1944 until June, Chief Bos'n Joseph Viera

1941 - War with Germany was imminent. The Coast Guard was transferred from the Treasury Department to the Navy in November 1941.

1942 - January 13th - Germans begin a U-boat offensive along east coast of USA.

1942 - January - A U.S. Navy torpedo bomber, making an emergency landing on North Beach, tore out its undercarriage and was recovered by the Navy using a flatbed truck and crane. This retrieval gear had to be towed by the Orleans and Old Harbor Station tractors from the Nauset Beach parking lot - several miles down the beach and back.

In March 1942, men on the station included Wilmer Doane, brothers Leland and James Williams, Russell Keith, Virgil Spaulding, Martin Connelly, John J. Murphy, John McKeon, Alphonse Zymball, and Henry Waserski. They were still practicing the Beach Apparatus drill, using #9 shot lines and two oz. of black powder in the Lyle gun. Pulling surfboat #4118, motor surfboat #4660 and tractor #1049 were in use. In August, the crew had stepped up surveillance and on the 2nd had "Examined & Checked Clearance papers of 21 motorboats".

Off the coast, enemy submarine activity was very effective in the first part of the war, and torpedoes sank many ships. An alert and suspicious Coast Guardsman had caught seven enemy saboteurs after their night landing on Long Island in the summer of 1942. Six were executed several months later. Beach patrols became intense.

Wartime measures instituted after that on the outer Cape included increased beach patrols that employed trained dogs. Lighthouses were extinguished, and black roller shades were employed in windows facing the sea so as not to create a silhouette of a ship for the German subs to target. Local fishermen were not allowed out during darkness.

In early 1944, top-secret plans were being drawn up for the D-Day invasion at Normandy, and Coast Guard resources would be needed to man landing craft and other vessels. In March, the crew included J. Kaiser, Wojcik, Miskell, O'Lear, Scherff, Beam, Gawronski, and Spaulding. Many Navy blimps and surface ships were recorded by the Station lookouts in the tower around this time, and enemy submarines had become less of a threat.

By April 1944, 800 men in New England were released from land-based patrol duties to sea duty. Old Harbor Station could not be adequately manned.

1944 – July 1 – The Station was officially decommissioned and closed. Many personnel files and logbooks were left behind.

Information in this chapter was obtained from the Annual Reports of The U.S. Life Saving Service; Annual Reports of The U.S. Coast Guard; the Inventory Log of Old Harbor Station; Old Harbor Station Rough Log Books; Coast Guard and Cape Cod National Seashore historical files, and newspaper articles as mentioned. Information about the dog patrol was taken from "Prints In The Sand - The U.S. Coast Guard Beach Patrol During World War II" by Eleanor C. Bishop.

CHAPTER 8

In Private Hands

The station was closed and boarded up, with the water pipes drained, in the summer of 1944. "Old Harbor stood abandoned for at least three years before it was privately purchased. The U.S. Government's Declaration of Abandonment was filed in Barnstable County on March 24, 1947. A bid to purchase the buildings had been made by Edwin Taylor and Jonathan Eldridge in September 1946. The two also acquired the land, which was not owned by the U.S. Government, from Oscar C. Nickerson. On August 30, 1948 the property was sold to Albert N. Long, although a property dispute 10 years later found that Oscar Nickerson held title to the land through adverse possession. After a final decree by the Superior Court of Massachusetts confirming Nickerson's title, a series of Quitclaim Deeds were filed. The property was transferred to Long, then to George Bearse and ultimately to Howard Rose. In 1959 Rose became joint owner, along with his wife and two daughters. In a letter, Rose said he purchased the buildings in 1948. Changes made to Old Harbor after the station was decommissioned are not well documented. It has been assumed that most if not all were instituted by Rose, who said he made "extensive alterations, repairs and improvements to not only the station but to the original stable building, workshop building and Boat House" immediately after acquiring the buildings and in later years.

According to Historical Architect Peggy Albee most of the alterations probably pre-date 1962, when the property was again offered for sale. The changes were geared toward transforming the station into a vacation retreat. Walls between the messroom, storm clothes closet, Keeper's office and stairway foyer were removed in order to create a single large living area. Walls were also removed around the pantry and between the rear entry and pantry to enlarge the kitchen. A shower was added to the first floor lavatory and a storage room was created in the southeast corner of the boat room. Screens were installed in the boatroom double doorways. On the second floor, what had been a single large sleeping room for the life saving crew, was divided into four bedrooms, although Albee suspects the southwest corner bedroom may have been created by the Coast Guard. A new bathroom and linen closet were added on the second floor. The boatroom loft was changed to a full floor over the span of the room, with a trap door and ladder for access. All floors were covered with linoleum or tile, except in the boatroom.

By 1962 the cellar had been partitioned into four distinct areas - a workshop, larder room, power plant and laundry area. Hot water was heated by gas and electricity was still provided by generators. In 1962 gas and electric space heaters were installed to supplement the limited warmth provided by the Heatilator fireplace in the former messroom. A combination of gas and electric lighting fixtures were being used in 1972, although it is not known when the gas fixtures were installed."

From *Volume 1, Historic Furnishings Report for Old Harbor Life-Saving Station*, prepared by Janice Hodson, March 2005. Courtesy of the Cape Cod National Seashore

Around 1946 or '47, David Ryder, a Chatham fisherman and son of former Officer in Charge Richard E. Ryder, purchased a small camp just to the north of the station. This was a fairly primitive place, having an outhouse, a coal burning cookstove, and a hand water pump. His family of four children (Nancy, John, author Richard, and Robert) absolutely loved being there. Understandably, his wife Alice did not. Access was by skiff from near the Chatham Fish Pier or by a modified Ford Model "B" 2WD beach buggy driven from Chatham via Orleans. Oversized tires, with air partially let out, made the travel possible.

L to R: Bob, John, Alice, & Richard Ryder.
Back row: Dot Wheeler, driver Dave Ryder, Nancy Ryder.

Many times, I am sure the women wished they were on the mainland. We boys entertained ourselves, as boys will. This included getting inside the boarded up station and exploring. In the kitchen and pantry, dried beans covered the floor. Attempts were made to climb the drill pole, as well as the steel weather bureau tower nearby. We played in the always cold surf unsupervised, and learned how to avoid rip currents.

The abandoned Life Saving Service and Coast Guard records and documents were strewn about the first floor. Looking back after 60+ years, I think it was a good thing that the building was unofficially accessible to so many people for several years. The record books were taken, not maliciously, but rather out of curiosity by many different parties, ultimately removed from the beach and stashed away as mementoes of an earlier time.

1968 Photo from author's collection

Old Harbor Station, with the Ryder Camp in foreground.

Decades later, as parents aged and the younger folks inherited "stuff", many of these invaluable record books have fortunately been donated to the Cape Cod National Seashore and are stored in climate-controlled conditions. They are accessible by prior arrangement with the Curator at the Salt Pond Visitor Center in Eastham.

During the Howard Rose era, many guests from New York and Connecticut enjoyed the Station. AppleJack brandy was the adult beverage of choice. The place had electricity and was relatively comfortable. Access for Howard and his guests was by his private plane or by boat. He hired local men as caretakers. One was Nate Higgins, seen (below) landing at the Chatham Fish Pier in the Old Harbor skiff. (Now the site of the Coast Guard dock.)

Postcard by Colourpicture Publishers, Boston

HOWARD ROSE AND THE OLD HARBOR STATION

"When Howard Rose, a summer visitor from Greenwich, Connecticut, came up just after World War II, he purchased the Old Harbor Station. This was in 1948. H. R. was a big hunter, fisherman, a great outdoorsman, so this place was pretty ideal. Howard bought a sizable chunk of land from one side to the other (ocean to bay), including the Boathouse on the bay side (also called the inside beach) and the two outbuildings, a workshop and a stable. Both buildings were to the south of the Old Harbor Station. H. R. was a plumbing contractor, college grad, and had a master's in engineering. He owned a large share in the plumbing company, Brant Jordan. If a school were being built, he would get the contract and do all the plumbing work. He was a reasonably well-off guy. The Old Harbor Station was quite a building. In the main building there was a huge kitchen with a restaurant stove that had six burners, two grills, and three or four ovens. There was also a living room and a bedroom on the first floor. A Boathouse was attached to the Station. This is where the surfboats were kept when it served as a lifesaving station. Upstairs were two bedrooms plus men's and ladies' rooms, each with two or three toilets plus showers. The stairway continued up to the tower. At this time at least two dunes were in front of the Station. From the tower you could see how the Cape bowed to the

NORTH BEACH FISHING LODGE
Chatham, Cape Cod, Mass.

Howard Rose's plane in the foreground. Old drill pole is at far left.
Postcard published for Mr. Rose by the Collotype Co., Elizabeth, NJ & NY

south. Howard fixed up the two outbuildings next to the station. He made two apartments in each building, small efficiency apartments with a sink, stove, and a refrigerator. He fixed these places up so his guests had a place to stay when they came over to visit for the weekend. This didn't work out very well because the guests ended up eating over at the Old Harbor Station. There was company there all the time. "

Photo taken from Howard Rose's plane.

"Chester Eldredge who lived in the camp next to the station with his wife Mamie became caretaker for the station after Howard bought it. Howard eventually bought the Eldredge's camp when Chester and Mamie moved back to the mainland. It was after Howard bought Chester's camp that he approached Nate Higgins about becoming caretaker for the Old Harbor Station. Nate, who was single at the time and working for Brant Jordan, agreed and lived right there at the station. Howard had guests come over for the weekend. They came from all over, and I don't think many really knew what type of place they were coming to. They came all dolled up in their city clothes, fur coats and all. Nate would get calls as late as 10:00 or 11:00 at night. They would have just flown into Chatham Airport and wanted to be picked up at the fish pier. This got old pretty quick. Getting up to go for a boat ride at this hour was not something to look forward to. When time and tide was right, Nate put an end to it. One night the water was rough. One of the passengers was a lady who always had her hair just so. Nate put the flat-bottomed boat into a wave and she got awfully wet to say the least. They never came back."

"Jack Kelly used to work at the airport in Chatham. He'd fly stuff over for Howard and land on the roadway next to the marsh. Eventually that road filled in and the flats to the north of the station on the bay side were used for landing. One time Howard ordered a dozen eggs; well, Jack brought over two dozen. He flew around and threw the first dozen at Howard, then landed and delivered the other dozen. "

From Drifting Memories – The Nauset Beach Camps On Cape Cod *by Frances L. Higgins*

Eventually, Howard must have realized that the land in front of his special place was eroding. He listed it for sale with Warrenton Williams of Eastham for $48,500.

"When the lodge was offered for sale in 1962 it was advertised as an "Oceanfront Sportsman's Paradise" with a sleeping capacity for 25 guests. Besides the original station building, two surviving out- buildings - the Life-Saving Service era stable and work- shop - had been remodeled as duplexes, each offering

Postcard of the New Bedford dragger *GLEN AND MARIA*, 10/19/65, ¹/₄ mile south of station

two one-and-a-half-room apartments with efficiency kitchens that included a General Chef combination refrigerator, stove and sink. Bathrooms with showers were on the first floors while the second floors of each apartment contained two bedrooms and a lavatory. The ad con- cluded that the site was "ideal for a sportsman's club, or a retreat for busy executives." By 1972, Rose was still seeking to sell but wished to retain rights to the buildings for 10 years and afterward donate the station structure to the Chatham Yacht Club. The property was not sold until 1973 when it was purchased by the National Park Service. "

From Volume 1, Historic Furnishings Report for Old Harbor Life-Saving Station, *prepared by Janice Hodson, March 2005. Courtesy of the Cape Cod National Seashore*

Old Harbor Station and out- buildings, about November 1970

Photo appeared in an MLS Ad in the *Cape Codder.* Photographer unknown

"INSIDE THE BOAT HOUSE

Note the 1919 capstan to the right, the gas lamps over the table, the propane refrigerator, and the ubiquitous bottle of Apple Jack brandy on the table. Bunk beds are to either side. Many guests, including the author, spent many pleasant evenings here over the years.

The Old Harbor Station boatroom converted to a game room for guests. Note the ping-pong table to the right, and the shuffleboard court markings on the floor.

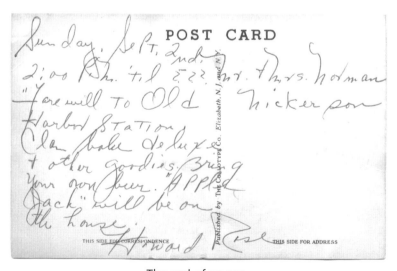

The end of an era.
Postcard sent to Mr. and Mrs. Norman Nickerson, nearby camp owners.

Sunday, September 2nd, 2:00 P.M. 'til ??? Farewell to Old Harbor Station.
Clam bake deluxe & other goodies. Bring your own beer. "Apple Jack" will be on the house.
Howard Rose

CHAPTER 9

Moving the Station - 1977

When Old Harbor Station was built in 1897, it was located on what was probably perceived to be comparatively firm ground. The site was high up on the beach; the end of the peninsula was between 500 and 1000 feet to the south; and the surf line was perhaps 300 feet east of the boatroom doors. The site selectors could not have known that in less than 80 years, the surf would be literally lapping at those doors, or that the end of the beach would be several miles to the south. The eastern shore of Cape Cod, locally known as the "back side", has been constantly eroding and changing since first being written about by Samuel DeChamplain in 1606. At one time, large sailing vessels could sail into Pleasant Bay without difficulty. However, sand from the outer beaches of Eastham and Orleans tends to be moved to the south by tidal currents and northeast storms. This movement gradually formed what is known as North Beach. At the time Old Harbor Station was built, the North Beach peninsula extended about six miles south from the mainland of Orleans, ending about due east of the present Chatham Fish Pier at the foot of Bar Cliff Avenue. The gradual diminishing of the distance from the boatroom ramp to the surf was not a cause for concern while

Photo by William P. Quinn

Old Harbor Station in the 1960s - Stable and workshop to left of main building. Note the amount of sand in front of building.

Photo by Dick Kelsey, Kelsey Airview - #77-819-4

August 19th, 1977 – Note how little sand is remaining now!

the station remained in service. After the station was closed in 1944, the relatively few people who visited the beach then of course noted the changes and remarked how much the beach had changed from their previous visit, but they had no major concerns. Mainland Chatham seemed secure, as did Old Harbor Station. The Winslow family of Orleans did lose a North Beach summer cottage to the sea during the late 1940s, but this event attracted little attention.

On June 22nd, 1973, the National Park Service purchased Old Harbor Station, and 19 acres surrounding it, from Howard Rose of Greenwich, Ct. for $44,935. The purchase was intended to bring more privately held property (located within the boundaries of the Cape Cod National Seashore) under the control of the Park Service, not necessarily to acquire more buildings. The high tide line at the time of purchase was no more than ten feet from the front door, and the Seashore Superintendent knew that the building was threatened. The building was proposed for inclusion in the National Register of Historical Places in 1975, but Superintendent Amberger had no money available to spend on moving it to a safer place. Moving the station to a spot closer to the bay side of North Beach was considered, but it was felt that the expenditure of money could not be justified. The Park Service wanted to use the building but it was so remote that relatively few visitors could get to it. It would be hard to ask Chatham residents to pay for moving the station to a location on the mainland when there was no site for it, and they certainly were not going to pay to have it moved out of town. In February of 1977, after a routine North Beach patrol, Chatham Police Lt. Barry Eldredge noted that the concrete apron in front of the boatroom had been undercut by the surf and had crumbled away. He felt that the next northeast storm would cause damage to the station itself. Things did not look good. In March, the Park Service was working on researching the station history, and meetings were being held to figure out what could be done with the building. In the July 20th issue of the *Cape Cod Times*, then Superintendent Hadley was quoted as saying, "Action must be taken between now and the fall storms if the structure is to be saved." In August 1977, the regional office of the Park Service was preparing an engineering plan for moving the station, and Mr. Hadley was feeling better about the chances for getting the needed funds.

It was at this time that a new, more stable site for the station, 200 yards from the Race Point parking lot in Provincetown, was announced. The plan was to move the station by floating it on a barge! Funds were finally made available under the historic preservation program of the National Park Service (North Atlantic Region), and a contract for $119,750.00 was awarded to Middlesex Contractors and Riggers of Lowell, Massachusetts on September 27, 1977. The first hurdle the contractor had to clear was the Chatham Conservation Commission. The contractor's original plan was to bring two 40-ton cranes and their associated moving equipment to the site by driving six miles over the beach roads from Orleans. Local residents wisely recognized the potential for damage to the dunes, and Commission member William Hammatt suggested that the equipment be ferried across the harbor by barge.

October 17, 1977 Storm (looking north)

Photo from Cape Cod National Seashore archives

West side of building, showing window coverings, porch braces, foundation pockets, and separation area between Boathouse and main building, November 6, 1977.

By the 2nd of November, one crane was sitting at Claflin Landing at Chatham, the other in town nearby. Things were about to happen. Moving the cranes across the harbor required the construction of a wooden ramp so the cranes could be driven onto a barge and taken over one at a time. Contractor Jack Corey of Middlesex Riggers hired Jackie Our and Hillard Hopkins to run an old Navy landing craft to tow the loaded barge, and after some difficulty in getting the barge afloat, Captain Our succeeded in moving the first crane across the harbor on Monday morning, November 7th. On Tuesday, the crane was moving across the sands of North Beach. The second crane and other equipment followed, and work began on separating the building into two sections.

By the 20th of November, the two cranes were shored up and in position on the north and south sides of the station, the boatroom had been separated from the other part of the building, and a steel lifting frame had been built under the building. Speculation abounded about whether or not the contractor could successfully lift the building, load it onto a barge in the surf, and get his expensive equipment clear of the area before a storm came up and ruined the whole project. Better than usual luck would have to be on the side of this optimistic Irishman.

The following description of the actual move was written by Philip K. Dodd & Charles C. Robb and appeared in the December 2nd, 1977 issue of *The Cape Codder*. "On Tuesday (November 29th), nine days after an earlier attempt was called off when the barge did not make it from Vineyard Haven, Jack Corey and his men put on a real show for several hundred

onlookers. The show had everything - drama, suspense, and derring-do by the Corey crew. It began around 11 am, when the barge arrived off the beach, under tow by the tug *TAURUS*. At the waters edge a bulldozer was running into the light surf, scooping out a landing area for the barge.

The dozen workmen had been at work since 7 am, making final preparations. At 11:40 Mr. Corey and several of his men revved up an amphibious "duck" (DUKW), loaded it with cable, and drove into the water to carry the cable to the waiting barge. The duck breasted the low breakers, headed out toward the barge, and then turned back. Someone had forgotten to leave one end of the cable ashore. The cable was secured to a bulldozer on the beach, and the duck started out again. Again it stopped short of the barge - the cable was too short. Another length was tied in ashore, the seaward end was at last secured to the barge, and a second bulldozer began to pull the barge shoreward. The cable dragged into a sand hump at the water's edge. A workman went to free it, and just as he arrived a wave broke high over the hump, dousing him. It was the start of a difficult day. Soon, however, the barge was ashore, snugged into its bulldozed berth, and the moving began. A window high in the station tower swung open and a man climbed onto the roof. It was John Brock, husband of the National Park Service's project director, Marsha Fader. Mr. Brock, assisted by his father, Albert Brock, strung three flags, the Stars and Stripes, a Coast Guard flag, and the orange, white and green flag of Ireland, provided by Mr. Corey. High tide was due around 2 pm, and the workers moved fast. First the boatroom section of the station, which had been separated from the main building, was lifted by one crane and swung aboard the shoreward end of the barge. It was necessary to move the boatroom to the seaward end of the barge to make room for the main building, and that proved to be a ticklish operation. Various maneuvers were tried, one of which involved a workman in an exhibition of aerial acrobatics worthy of Barnum & Bailey, as he grappled heavy cables to join the gigantic hooks of the two cranes. By artful crane work, the boat-room on its underpinning of steel girders was jockeyed to the outer end of the barge, and attention turned to the main stage – the station itself. Each of the 40-ton cranes hooked a side of the station. Their motors roared, but the station did not budge. On one of the cranes the gears were slipping. A workman scooped a shovelful of sand, clambered into the engine room and poured sand onto the gears (or clutch). Again the engines roared. Loud crunches were heard, as the station rose from its foundation, and the 80-year connection was broken.

Cheers filled the air, and Mr. Corey, standing on the barge, guided the 60-ton station towards the water with subtle hand signals to his two crane operators. Meanwhile Chatham fisherman Jackie Our kept his World War II landing craft pushing the barge shoreward to keep it steady. All 90 feet of the barge were taken up when the station was gently dropped on. The station was blocked up, cables were lashed down, and the steel beams welded securely to the barge. Finally at 4 pm, with darkness setting in, an attempt was made to push the barge off, but the tide had left it high and almost dry. The two bulldozers lined up and started pushing. The tug and the landing craft started pulling. The barge didn't budge. Mr. Corey conferred with his subcontractor and the decision was made to wait until the next high tide, at about 2 am. Even then, the barge proved balky, and Mr. Corey and his crew had to improvise a new tactic. The crane booms were lowered on each side of the barge and the cables connected under the landward end of the barge.

Loading the main building on the barge, November 29th, 1977

With the cranes pulling and the bulldozers pushing, the barge began to inch away. It was finally off the beach at 3 am, but then it grounded on a sandbar. The dozers started to build a bridge out to the sandbar to push some more, but the tug then earned its name, *TAURUS*, and pulled the barge off by itself. The tow to Provincetown went smoothly, and by 9 am, November 30th, Old Harbor Station was off Race Point, its next and final destination. The landing must await the dismantling and moving of the cranes from North Beach to Race Point."

An older mariner, seeing the barge underway with its unusual cargo, is supposed to have remarked "I've cruised by a lot of Coast Guard stations during my lifetime, but this is the first time I've ever seen a Coast Guard station cruise by me!"

Rounding Long Point at Provincetown, November 30th, 1977

Barge tied up in Provincetown Harbor, late 1977

After the actual lifting of the station and moving of the barge to Provincetown Harbor was completed, the contractor moved his cranes back to the mainland, removed the old foundation, backfilled the holes, and rebuilt the dunes that were necessarily altered by the moving operation. Beach grass was later planted to stabilize the affected beach. A visitor to the site today would not know that a building ever stood there.

After several postponements due to construction problems and adverse weather (including the February "Blizzard of '78"), the station was placed on land again in May of 1978.

The following account of the unloading first appeared in the May 20th issue of *The Cape Cod Times*. "It loomed up first at 8:30 Friday morning, a darker place in the fog at Race Point, then gradually resolved into the by now familiar shape of the Old Harbor Coast Guard station on its barge. But the work had already started. "Fat Allis" (built by the Fiat Allis Co.), the biggest bulldozer on Cape Cod, had been busy since long before daylight. It was scooping out what amounted to a small harbor for the barge, piling sand up on each side. Jack Corey's two giant cranes were already busy laying heavy timber pads on top of those sand jetties to get as close to the barge as they could. It was still too early, since the tide wasn't due to be high for at least another hour. Slowly, as the tug *TAURUS* from Vineyard Haven, and Ralph Andrews' Provincetown dragger *PETREL* applied the power, the building became an apparition again, dissolving back into the fog. Fifteen minutes later, again out of the mist came the old building on its barge, this time to stay.

Old Harbor Life-Saving Station appearing out of the fog of May 19, 1978, after being towed from Provincetown Harbor to Race Point.

"It still would be two hours before all would be ready, though. The welds had to be burned off. Those welds had held the steel platform the station had rested on since its lift off from North Beach in Chatham last November. Extra weights had to be added to the two cranes, outriggers made secure, slings rigged. A trial lift was made. Something was stuck on one corner of the old building. Then, almost as if the gods were smiling at that one spot on the beach, the fog cleared, the sun came out, and just before 11 am, the two cranes put a strain on the slings, revved their big diesels, and slowly, slowly, the 81-year old structure lifted off the barge. It slowly twisted in the air, straightened, and the two crane operators working in tandem but unseen by each other, employing some arcane form of telepathic communication, swung their giant booms inward - slowly, slowly - and lowered. Old Harbor Station, five months and 28 days after it had left Chatham, was on dry land once more. There followed several more hours of work as the boatroom, severed from the main building last fall, was landed alongside the main building. While the station is now on the beach, it will take several more lifts before it is set on cribbing over the foundation footings several feet inland from where it was first set down. According to Marsha Fader, National Park Service architectural historian who has directed the project from the beginning, the foundation will be built up to the building, based on how far out of plumb the old structure is. According to Fader, however, no funds are currently budgeted for restoration of the building, and the immediate concern is to make the structure sound and tight."

Lifting building onto shore at Race Point, May 19, 1978

Kelsey Airviews are available from Kelsey-Kennard Photographers, 465 Main Street, Chatham, MA. 02633.
www.capecodphotos.com

CHAPTER 10

Rebuilding the Station

"Under the direction of National Park Service (NPS) Historical Architect Marsha Fader, Old Harbor Station was moved by barge to Provincetown harbor in November 1977. The station had to be sawed in half, the chimney dismantled and most of the original plaster ceilings removed to reduce weight to facilitate the move. The move itself was unprecedented in NPS history. The final project cost was $118,578.59. Due to project overruns, restoration carpentry work on the station, originally part of the contract, was undertaken instead by the NPS in-house staff. Between August 1978 and November 1980 work proceeded fitfully. The first floor rooms were restored (with the exception of the floors themselves) and limited work was done on the second floor. All work accomplished, including shingling, plastering, re-erecting interior walls, constructing boat ramps, rebuilding of the front and rear porches, was done based on a combination of remaining physical evidence and the original 1897 building specifications. The reproduction doors for the boatroom were made to slide, not swing as they did after 1910; the west doorway of the boatroom, which had been blocked since 1910, was reopened; the interior paint colors used on the first floor and stairwell levels were matched to the tones found in the first paint layers dating no later than 1899. At the time the Historic Structure Report was written in 1988, much of the restoration work was incomplete, particularly on the second floor. Vandals had destroyed part of the work done on the first floor. Work on the structure between 1988 and 2006 has primarily been to address preservation problems. Severe storms and driving rain often infiltrated the building and periodic break-ins resulted in structural damage. Following a storm in October 1991, water infiltrated the boatroom through a broken window, around the ocean side doors and through a roof leak above the surfboat. The floor of the crew's sleeping quarters on the second floor contained 1 1/2" of water and a leak in the tower stairwell was described as "severe". Recommendations made by the Buildings Conservation Branch in 1995 for rectifying roof leaks testify to the persistence of this particular problem."

Excerpted from the Historic Furnishings Report for Old Harbor Lifesaving Station, Volume 1 *, prepared for the Park Service in 2005 by Janice Hodson*

The North District Interpretive Staff has managed to hold successful Open Houses at the station in the summer, as well as conduct the popular Beach Apparatus Drills on Thursday evenings.

Between 2001 and 2002, the Northeast Buildings Conservation Center oversaw the installation of a new roof, rehabilitation of the sliding boatroom doors and window sashes. By 2004, a sprinkler system was installed throughout the building. There is no running water at the Station, so this system is pressurized with an antifreeze solution that is stored in large tanks in the basement.

In 2008, major funding for completion of the restoration was received. The objective is to portray the building as it appeared in the years from 1900 to perhaps 1908. Cape Cod National Seashore carpenters started work during the summer of 2008, working around the schedule of the Interpretive Rangers. This painstaking, detailed work consisted of patching many holes in the subfloor and finish floors, fitting beaded vertical pieces in the knee wall areas of the second floor, and construction of replica crew lockers in the second floor hallway. Repairs to plaster walls were started. The carpenters will be constructing replica shelving in the Messroom as well as performing numerous other repairs to wood trim.

Photo from the author's collection

Here, work on framing in the area under the eaves in the spare room is progressing.

Photos by the author

Here is one of the many holes in the floor that had to be patched. This one was in the second floor spare room, where there once had been a toilet. Original vertical grain yellow pine flooring taken from under the eaves was reused where appropriate. In some areas, fir flooring had to be procured to match the original.

In 2009, contractors have reshingled the exterior walls and painted the trim. Much credit should go to the Cape Cod National Seashore staff for pursuing the funding and for carrying out the restoration in such a fine manner.

Larry Seaboyer and Paul Schneider, Seashore finish carpenters

CHAPTER 11

The Future of Old Harbor Station

The good news is that the dunes near the station continue to build up, thus ensuring that the building is not in any danger from the sea, at least for now.

In 2009, the Cape Cod National Seashore has scheduled the following interior work: finishing the shelving in the messroom; further repairs to the trim; repainting certain areas; and sanding and oiling of the first and second story wood floors. The old growth southern yellow pine and fir will then take on a wonderful honey color.

If restoration funds are remaining, a new elevated exterior walkway will be constructed that will allow visitors to safely walk between the shore and the front of the building. This will enhance the visitor experience in that they'll see another face of the building, and perhaps they will be able to see the ocean.

In 2005, the Seashore received *Volume Two of the Historic Furnishings Report for the Old Harbor Lifesaving Station*. This rather detailed study, the "Implementation Plan", outlines several options as to how the station will ultimately be furnished. There are scale drawings of each room, along with numbered sketches of proposed objects and written descriptions of these items. What will be in the Messroom, The Boatroom, the Keeper's Office, etc.? *Volume Two* has it all spelled out, almost like getting a MapQuest printout! The Interpretive Staff has advocated using replica furnishings when possible, as the station is remote and security of original artifacts could be a problem. In my estimation, the major items needed that would enhance the visitor experience would be a wagon for the surfboat, a messroom table and chairs, and a coal burning cookstove for the kitchen. Plans and or specifications for these items are available.

In the near future, the newly renovated second floor will become accessible. Perhaps an Interpretive Ranger will explain aspects of a Surfman's life, while downstairs another Ranger or volunteer will enlighten visitors. The Friends of the Cape Cod National Seashore (www.fccns.org) have agreed to mount a campaign to raise money for acquiring furnishings. This is an ongoing project that has been delayed due to the building interior not being completed. There is no problem in determining what used to be in the building, as the original Inventory Logbook exists that covers all the items that were ever received at the station from 1898 until 1922. In addition, the Park Service has listings of original equipment provided in 1898, as well as forms called "Returns of Public Property", which are basically inventory lists made out periodically by the Keeper to verify what was on hand.

When the long-range plans of the Cape Cod National Seashore come to fruition, we'll see the Station more completely furnished with equipment and artifacts that accurately depict life at the Station around 1900. It will be wonderful to see an original Duluth style station in such starkly beautiful surroundings.

It will be an American experience only possible on Cape Cod!

Acknowledgements

The author wishes to thank the Ryder family, for their contributions and support; Glenn Stockwell, Nautical historian of Eastham, for his diligent research; Mary Ann Gray, Archivist of the Chatham Historical Society, for her assistance; Hope Morrill, Curator, Cape Cod National Seashore, for her help in locating photos and documents; Nancy Viall Shoemaker, proprietor, West Barnstable Press, for her exceptional creativity and cooperation; historian and author Bill Quinn for his help with photographs; Frances L. Higgins, author of *Drifting Memories*, for her support; Shirley Sabin for her meticulous proofreading; and lastly, my wife and friend Patricia, whose encouragement, guidance, and patience the past two decades is most appreciated.

Bibliography

ALLIS-CHALMERS Data Book, Terry Dean, Motorbooks International, 2000

ANNUAL REPORTS OF THE U.S. COAST GUARD, Government Printing Office, 1915 - 1922; U.S. Coast Guard Academy Library, New London, Ct.

ANNUAL REPORTS OF THE U.S. LIFE SAVING SERVICE, Government Printing Office, 1896 - 1914; U.S. Coast Guard Academy Library, New London, Ct.

A PILGRIM RETURNS TO CAPE COD by Edward Rowe Snow; The Yankee Publishing Co. 1946

BEACH APPARATUS DRILL, U.S. Government Printing Office, 1918

CAPE COD YESTERDAYS, by Joseph C. Lincoln; Little, Brown & Co., 1937

CHATHAM - "THE LIFEBOATMEN", by Bernard C. Webber; Lower Cape Publishing, Orleans, 1985

DARRY THE LIFE SAVER, or The Heroes of The Coast, by Frank V. Webster; Cupples & Leon, 1911

DRIFTING MEMORIES, The Nauset Beach Camps on Cape Cod, by Frances L. Higgins, Lower Cape Publishing, Orleans, 2004

EAST OF CAPE COD, by Asa Paine Lombard, Jr.; privately published, 1976

FIGHTING THE SEA, or Winter At The Life-Saving Station, by Edward A. Rand; Thomas W. Whittaker, 1887

FROM HIGHLAND TO HAMMERHEAD – The Coast Guard and Cape Cod, by Captain Charles B. Hathaway, U.S.C.G., 2000

GUARDSMEN OF THE COAST, by John J. Floherty; The Junior Literary Guild, 1935

HISTORIC STRUCTURE REPORT for OLD HARBOR STATION, by Peggy Albee, National Park Service, 1988

HISTORIC FURNISHINGS REPORT for OLD HARBOR LIFE-SAVING STATION, Volume 1, Historical Data, by Janice Hodson, National Park Service, 2005

HISTORIC FURNISHINGS REPORT for OLD HARBOR LIFE-SAVING STATION, Volume 2, Implementation Plan, by Janice Hodson, National Park Service, 2005

INSTRUCTIONS FOR U.S. COAST GUARD STATIONS, Government Printing Office, 1922

INSTRUCTIONS TO MARINERS IN CASE OF SHIPWRECK, Government Printing Office, 1881

INVENTORY LOG OF OLD HARBOR LIFE-SAVING STATION, 1898 – 1922, Author's Collection

Bibliography (cont'd)

LIFE SAVING NANTUCKET, by Edouard A. Stackpole; Nantucket Life Saving Museum, 1972

LOG BOOKS OF OLD HARBOR STATION, 1898 - 1941; National Archives, Waltham, MA; Record Group 26, Boxes 298 - 304

MODERN SEAMANSHIP, by Rear Admiral Austin M. Knight, U.S. Navy; Van Nostrand Co., 1918

PRINTS IN THE SAND, The U.S. Coast Guard Beach Patrol During WW II, by Eleanor C. Bishop, Pictorial Histories Publishing Co., 1989

RECOLLECTIONS OF BENJAMIN O. ELDREDGE; Oral History Cassette Tape done in 1965 by Ken Matteson; Chatham Historical Society

RECOLLECTIONS OF REBECCA DAVIS SMITH RYDER; Oral History Cassette Tape done in April 1978; Mystic Seaport Museum, Mystic, Ct.

ROUGH LOGS from the Tower of Old Harbor, various years; Author's Collection

RUGGED WATER, by Joseph C. Lincoln; D. Appleton & Co., 1924

SURFBOATS, ROCKETS, AND CARRONADES, by CDR Robert F. Bennett, U.S.C.G; Government Printing Office, 1976

SURFMEN AND LIFESAVERS, by Paul Giambarba; The Scrimshaw Press, 1985

THE AMERICAN LIFE-SAVING SERVICE - 1880, by J.H. Merryman; *Harpers Magazine*, 1882

THE ARCHITECTURE OF U.S. LIFE-SAVING STATIONS, by Wick York; The LOG, Mystic Seaport Museum, 1982

THE BEACH PATROL, by William Drysdale; W. A. Wilde & Co., ca. 1899

THE DORY BOOK, by John Gardner; International Marine Publishing Co., 1978

THE LIFEBOAT AND ITS' STORY, by Noel T. Methley; J.B. Lippincott, 1912

THE LIFE SAVERS OF CAPE COD, by J.W. Dalton; Barta Press, 1902

THE LIFESAVING GUNS OF DAVID LYLE, by J.P. Barnett; South Bend Replicas, Inc., 1976

THE UNITED STATES LIFE-SAVING SERVICE; *Scribner's Monthly*, January 1880

THE UNITED STATES LIFE-SAVING SERVICE, by W.D. O'Connor Ass't. Superintendent, U.S.L.S.S.; Appleton & Co., 1889

TREASURES OF THE SHORE, A Beachcomber's Botany, by Marcia Norman; The Chatham Conservation Foundation, Inc., 1963

ABOUT THE AUTHOR

Richard G. Ryder is a descendant of some of the earliest families to settle in Chatham on Cape Cod. Many of his ancestors made their living around the shores or at sea, and he was raised in Chatham close to the sounds of the surf and lightship foghorns. His family had a camp near Old Harbor Station, and he spent many happy hours of his youth walking the nearby beaches. He has long been interested in the history of the U. S. Life Saving Service and has a varied collection of associated memorabilia.

His website (www.uslifesavingmarker.com) is devoted to former Surfmen and Keepers. His grandfather was a Surfman in the Life Saving Service and eventually became the Keeper at Old Harbor. His father David F. Ryder, a retired Chatham fisherman, was a highly respected Selectman of that town.

Richard is a retired Navy officer, having spent 20 years in the Medical Department. He is a graduate of Stockbridge School of Agriculture and Cornell University. He has built five small wooden boats. His interests include the operation and maintenance of the historic Coast Guard motor lifeboat CG36500 (www.CG36500.org), Nauset Lighthouse (www.nausetlight.org), and assisting the National Park Service in interpreting the Old Harbor Station for summer visitors to the Cape Cod National Seashore.

His first book, "Old Harbor Station – Cape Cod" was published in 1990 and is out of print.

This book was printed on 70 lb. opaque white offset and 10 pt. Kromekote which was laminated on one side. It was designed and typeset by Nancy Viall Shoemaker of West Barnstable Press. Palatino was the predominant font used - for the text and chapter heads. Palatino was designed by Hermann Zapf in 1948 with an appreciaton of the graceful calligraphy of 16th century Italian calligrapher Giambattista Palatino. Captions and image credits were set in Frutiger, a classic of contemporary typography. Adrian Frutiger (b. 1928 Zurich) developed this font in 1975. With modifications, it has become one of the most popular sans serif types and is used almost exclusively on municipal signs in Switzerland. On page 100, Kid Print (1998 by Monotype) was used for the message on the post card.